Is It True What They Say About Black Men?
Copyright ©2014 by Jeremy Helligar

All rights reserved. No portion of this book may be reproduced or transmitted in any form or by any means, electronic or mechanical, including photocopying, recording, or by any information storage and retrieval system without written permission from the author, except for the inclusion of brief quotations in a review.

First Edition 2014

Cover Photo:
Russell Smith

Cover Design:
Craig Keown, Frederick Peens

Copy Editor:
Marla Garfield

IS IT TRUE WHAT THEY SAY ABOUT BLACK MEN?

Tales of Love, Lust and Language Barriers
on the Other Side of the World

Jeremy Helligar

To Lori: Thank you for holding my hand from the other side of the world and making me believe my stories were worth telling.

Time + Travel: Places and Faces

2007
Buenos Aires (Hernán, Lucas, Marcelo)

2008
Buenos Aires (the "taxi boy")

2009
Buenos Aires (Alvaro, Gejo)

2010
Buenos Aires ("G")
Melbourne (Clint, Shane)

2011
Buenos Aires
Melbourne (Shane, Clint, Nathan)
Sydney (Tomas)
Auckland
Bangkok (Marc, Mark)
Phnom Penh
Siem Reap
Manila (Malcolm)
Pattaya (Alan)
Koh Chang

2012
Melbourne (Shane)
Bangkok (Jack, "G," Edward, Rudie, Jorge, Andrew, Shane)
Chiang Mai
Krabi (Andrew)

2013
Melbourne (Shane, Marty, Clint, Nicholas)
Berlin
Rome
Tel Aviv
Johannesburg
Cape Town (Gejo)

Prologue: Searching

You get what you're not looking for. The best things in life aren't necessarily free (you get what you pay for, too), but they're often completely unexpected: love, friendship, the perfect job, a stunning view, a grand epiphany. Oh, the thrill of happy accidents, things you stumble upon when you're looking for something else, or when you aren't looking at all.

I had no idea what I was looking for when I launched my expat adventure around the world. I'd always been driven by wanderlust, so traveling was in my soul. I'd spent years dreaming of being born again, rising from corporate journalism's golden coffin lined with biweekly paycheck stubs and 401K receipts, and relocating to a land far, far away. I didn't think I'd ever actually do it, though. Where would I put all of my stuff?

After fifteen years as a magazine writer and editor in New York City, I was feeling restless and craving change. I loved my job, but I hated my work. As much as I respected the publications for which I had toiled over the years (*People*, *Teen People*, *Us Weekly*, *Entertainment Weekly*), I felt like a hack. I was doing it for the money, and I wasn't making enough of it to distract me from the bigger picture.

I wanted to write about something more meaningful than baby bumps, PDA and who was sleeping in Britney Spears's bed, but I wasn't sure how to reinvent myself. The first thing they teach you in journalism school is to "write what you know." I knew a lot about music, movies, pop culture and celebrities. But I didn't really know anything at all.

I needed a new classroom. New York City had been good to me. I made decent money, and I owned a great apartment in an ideal location, on 14th Street, right off Union Square. I was at the center of the universe, surrounded by friends and colleagues. But I felt so alone. In my twenties, I'd had three significant relationships (with Derek, Khleber and Tommy) that each lasted for around one year. My thirties were defined by short romances (with Todd, Kevin, Khleber again, Bryan-with-a-*y*), none lasting longer than a few months, and one-night stands, each less fulfilling than the one before it.

"Why don't you have boyfriend?"

That question was the bane of my bachelorhood in New York City, frequently asked by concerned friends and curious strangers. Why *was* I still single? I have four theories.

1. Living in New York City is not conducive to long-term romance. Anyone who has seen *Sex and the City* knows that. And being a salty, cynical Miranda (with the occasional Samantha rising) didn't do my love life any favors.
2. I was a black man in a white gay world. Therefore, I was largely invisible. I wasn't what most American gay men, white or black, were looking for, which came as quite a surprise to a black woman who started talking to

me one night at the Cock, a raunchy sex dive on Avenue A in the East Village. She couldn't understand why I was standing on my own, watching men walk right past me to line up to get to Dave, my white, blue-eyed best friend. "Everyone here should be all over *you*," she insisted. "The gay men in New York City must either be blind or racist as hell." By way of commiseration and flattery, she had nailed an undeniable urban truth.

3. I was too picky. On the day I turned twenty-eight, my mother, Dave and I were on our way to my birthday dinner in Tribeca when the subject turned to my chronically pitiful romantic status. Mom offered her own theory to explain it: "You give up on people too easily." I didn't see it her way — not entirely. I just didn't have the patience to cling to a relationship that clearly wasn't working in hopes that it one day might. She didn't raise no fool for love.
4. I didn't really know what I was doing.

My sister once shared an interesting quote with me: "Men need to make love to feel love. Women need to feel love to make love." What nobody ever told me was that men need to have intercourse to feel like they're making love. In some ways, I was practically a virgin. I'd lived in New York City for fifteen years and traveled all over Europe and, somehow, I had escaped that dreaded "Top or bottom?" question. I had no idea what I wasn't missing.

I could have counted on one hand the number of men with

whom I went all the way during my first decade and a half of gay sexual activity, which began at age twenty-two with Ken, also twenty-two, whom I met at a long-defunct East Village gay watering hole called Tunnel Bar, a few weeks into my life as a new New Yorker. He was the first guy I ever let inside of me (with a condom, of course, for I was an obedient child of the safe-sex era) and the last in New York City to request entry via the back door.

    Most of my boyfriends and the men I hooked up with didn't seem to be any more interested in anal sex than I was. For me, it was too painful as a "bottom," too boring as a "top." I certainly wasn't going to initiate it, and the men I met didn't either. Maybe the fear of HIV and AIDS and the still somewhat primitive treatments discouraged them from pursuing intercourse with the wild abandon that was to come, but I can't help but wonder how many of them must have left my bedroom disappointed, determined never to return.

    It wasn't until I moved to Buenos Aires that I realized how crucial penetration and sex roles were to gay love and romance, for horny Argentines, especially the twentysomething ones who came of age during the era of HIV drug therapies, when being positive was no longer a death sentence, were nothing if not forthcoming and sexually reckless. The gay world there was divided into two types: *activos y pasivos* ("tops and bottoms"), especially for the latter. The "bottoms" seemed to be the majority and, for the most part, they were interested only in what you could give them. The blacker, the bigger (according to that old urban myth, which they embraced with lustful gusto). The bigger, the better! I'd traded one fringe existence for another!

The feeling of forever being an outsider and the sense of isolation that came with it was what had led me to Buenos Aires in September of 2006. (My aforementioned "stuff" went into a Brooklyn storage space.) After so many years in New York City, I still didn't know where I fit in there, as a human being, as a journalist, as a gay man, as a black man.

I'd had a lifelong complicated relationship with people of my own color. It began when I was four years old and my family moved from the U.S. Virgin Islands, where I was born, to the U.S. mainland, in Kissimmee, Florida, where I would spend my fourteen most formative years. We eventually settled in an all-black neighborhood, and despite the physical similarities I shared with our neighbors, I probably wouldn't have felt more like an outsider if we'd ended up in the whitest part of town.

The racism that Kissimmee's white redneck population directed toward me didn't compare to the racism and xenophobia I encountered from the black Americans there who resented my family because we were black and foreign. They called us "noisy Jamaicans" because, apparently to them, one Caribbean island fit all. We spoke with strange accents, and we kept to ourselves. Who did we think we were? What did we think we were: better than them?

When my first-grade classmates asked me where I was from because of the funny way I spoke (counting to "tree" instead of three), I sometimes lied and said the Virginia Islands, hoping they wouldn't realize that no such thing existed. I was too ashamed to say "the Virgin Islands." I wanted to fit in, and if the way I talked was going to lead to ostracism by my black classmates (interestingly, I can't recall a single white kid ever ridiculing me for that), at least I could come from a place that wasn't so exotic.

White bullies limited their racism to verbal cut-downs. It never touched me physically. "I smell nigger" coming from rednecks on the playground damaged my eleven-year-old psyche, but the black-on-black racism left physical as well as emotional scars. If they thought their words could never hurt me, the black bullies started picking up sticks and stones.

The physical bruises healed, but the mental ones never did completely. It wasn't until I went to the University of Florida in Gainesville that I finally escaped the emotional and physical cruelty. For the first time, the majority of black Americans I met didn't treat me like the enemy. If my exposure to them helped me to eventually overcome the fear and resentment of black people that had been borne from my experiences in Kissimmee, I never forgot how difficult and confusing it had been to be one of them, a so-called African-American, while not being accepted as one of them.

I didn't set out to write a book. I just started writing —

long emails to friends in which I shared my travel tales, articles for various magazines and websites, entries in Theme for Great Cities, the travel / entertainment / lifestyle blog that I launched in 2008. It was my blog readers — a combination of old and new friends, family members, former colleagues and people I'd never met — who convinced me to compile my experiences as a stranger in strange lands negotiating love, lust and racism in new cultural settings and in different languages into a book. (The names of most lovers and other strangers have been changed to protect their privacy.)

   I had stories to tell the world. I also had bills to pay. Freelance writing doesn't guarantee you'll earn enough money to get around any city, much less around the world. I was fortunate enough to have done relatively well financially. When I traded New York City for Buenos Aires, I had two apartments — one in the city I was leaving, one in my destination — to show for my decade and a half of professional effort. I lived mostly off my savings and rental income from the one in New York City for my first three years in Buenos Aires, before selling it in late 2009 and dialing 1-800-GOT-JUNK to arrange for the disposal of most of my mostly forgotten stuff, which was now officially "junk," in the Brooklyn storage space for a $500 fee. The tidy profit from the apartment sale continues to finance my expatriation.

   Meanwhile, I perfected the art of living on $10 to $15 a

day, which was fairly easy in cheap cities where the U.S. dollar was strong, like Buenos Aires and Bangkok, but a considerable challenge in overpriced Melbourne. The money you save by not eating out, not being a slave to the latest fashion and not accumulating new possessions you can put toward other nonessentials, like plane tickets.

The rest you just improvise. I didn't intend to spend four and a half years in Buenos Aires. I'd gone there on my three previous holidays and bought a one-bedroom apartment in Palermo on the third one, so it seemed like an excellent time to put it to good use. I arrived for the fourth time expecting to last six months there. Four years later, in 2010, I visited Australia for the first time with tentative plans to make Sydney my new home and fell in love with Melbourne instead. I went to Bangkok for one month only in July of 2012 and ended up spending a total of seventeen months there during the next two years.

You get what you're not looking for. I knew that when I set sail from one "New World" to another. I was hoping that somehow, unexpectedly, I'd find it.

I. Scenes of the Crimes

Thieves in the Temple

Most people get one defining moment in life — a split second, an hour, a day, maybe a week or longer — when something happens, and they know things will never again be the same. I've had two. The first was September 11, 2001, the day I watched the second tower of the World Trade Center go down, seemingly in slow motion, from the vantage point of Avenue of the Americas in New York City.

The other day that will live in infamy? February 18, 2007, the day I was robbed in my apartment in Buenos Aires by three men, at screwdriver-point. Yes, that's right: assault with a deadly screwdriver!

It was a beautiful sunny summer afternoon, a Sunday five months and two days into my self-imposed exile from New York City and relocation to Buenos Aires. I was returning home in Palermo Hollywood after picking up my once-every-weekend comfort-food lunch (a cheese omelet, french fries and freshly squeezed orange juice) at my favorite neighborhood café, thinking about how lucky I was that, after fifteen years of being surrounded by hustle, bustle and concrete in the Big Apple, I was living a brand-new domestic dream in the one-bedroom apartment I had bought the year before on one of the many quiet *calles* in BA (as its local expats called my newly adopted hometown) that were lined with trees in full seasonal bloom. They extended upward and forward from the edge of the pavement on opposite sides of the roads, like leafy, green military lines, creating a chiaroscuro cathedral effect that was most stunning in the early morning when the sunlight was just starting to peek through.

Thank God it was several blocks removed from Avenida Santa Fe's Manhattan-level pollution (only worse than Manhattan's), its architectural hodgepodge of white, beige, brown and red brick — commercial and residential spaces that sprouted from the city's broken sidewalks and encompassed glossy new five-star constructions alternating with shabby '70s-style buildings in desperate need of a soapy rain shower with bleach. At certain street-level vantage points, from a viewing distance of a hundred meters or more, they almost seemed to be reaching toward each other from across the frequently traffic-jammed *avenida* as they ascended heavenward to the clear blue skies.

I was in a fantastic mood, mid-reverie, daydreaming about the gorgeous twenty-five-year-old lawyer I'd met the night before while clubbing with Hernán, my Argentine friend with occasional benefits, at Glam. The lawyer had left my place just a little while ago. Had I finally struck hookup gold after months of kissing toads? What would I wear for our date that evening?

When the elevator opened on the sixth floor, I stepped out and noticed that the door to my apartment was open. A man was standing there, in front of my place, waiting. Two others crossed the threshold into the hallway. They were dressed in maintenance-worker blue, so at first, I assumed there was some problem in my apartment, perhaps a leak, and the super had let them in so they could fix it. Construction of the eight-story building had been completed only a couple of months earlier, and most of the apartments in it were still unoccupied.

The men began motioning for me not to say a word, covering their mouths with their index fingers as they approached me. Obviously, this was no maintenance call, but I still didn't understand what was happening, so I continued trying to come up with explanations in my head. Had they received a tip that there was a burglar in my apartment? Were they about to pounce on him and didn't want to give themselves away? Yes, a ridiculous assumption, and I sort of knew it at the time, but in this potentially dangerous defining moment, my mind worked in mysterious and not necessarily rational ways, leading to responses that I never would have predicted five minutes earlier.

When they grabbed me and dragged me over the threshold and into the apartment, I reconsidered. Maybe this was a racially motivated hate crime. I'd been told that despite appearances — lustful *porteños*, as the native citizens of BA referred to themselves, fawning over the new black man in town — Argentines had a strong racist streak. But these burglars had broken into my apartment before I'd arrived home. How could they have known anything about my demographic profile? They'd seemed genuinely surprised when the elevator door opened a few moments earlier. Clearly, they weren't expecting a tall black guy to step off. It wasn't like there were many of us running around town!

Maybe my uninvited houseguests were part of some terrorist plot to kidnap American expatriates in BA and sell them into *gringo* slavery. Hadn't I seen that in an action movie once? No, I couldn't have. I was always more into indie dramas and art-house character studies. I'd seen Jodie Foster in *Panic Room* and *Flight Plan,* though. I knew I had to kick ass and save my butt.

So I fought back, battling burglars and odds that were stacked against me: three (them) to one (me). It wasn't fair. But neither was life. If it were, I still would have been daydreaming about my handsome lawyer.

At the time, I'd been taking private Spanish lessons only for a few months, so I still spoke very little Spanish and couldn't make out what the intruders were saying. But if a picture is worth a thousand words, the sight of one of them threateningly holding a screwdriver over my face was worth a million. None of those words, however, could possibly describe my fear, nor were any needed to incite it. That screwdriver told me all I needed to know.

So I fought harder. Soon we were on the bathroom floor, struggling. I looked out of the window above the bidet and toilet and thought about my mother. Although we had not been on speaking terms for more than a year, I couldn't do this to her. She'd already lost one child, my sister, who died in infancy a few years before I was born. Although Mom never really talked about Josie Ann, all of my life, whenever I looked at her and noticed a faraway look in her eyes, I always assumed she was thinking about the daughter and sister neither one of us ever got to know.

I couldn't die on my bathroom floor in a pool of blood. It was fight or fright, and while I couldn't avoid the latter, I was going to embrace the former. I managed to get the screwdriver from the guy who was taunting me with it, grabbing it by the blade (securing myself a permanent scar between the index and middle finger of my left hand in the process) and tossing the weapon behind the toilet.

They'd taken my belts from my closet, and the one who'd been wielding the screwdriver began to tie one of them into a noose. Oh no! My mind raced to the worst place imaginable: They were going to hang me from the shower curtain rod! Never mind that it was adjustable: As I already pointed out, this was not the time for rational thinking.

Just when I began to fear that maybe it was all over for me, I had an epiphany: They weren't out to kill me. Come on, I thought, this is three against one. If they wanted to eliminate me, they would have done so by now. They were robbing me! They were *fucking* robbing me!

"Take what you want!" I shouted. "And get the fuck out of here!" Bastards!

They seemed to understand. Once I stopped struggling, they used one of my belts to tie my feet together and another to tie my hands behind my back. Then they gagged me with the pink bandana I kept tied around the handle on my suitcase to set it apart from the others on the airport carousel whenever I traveled.

They wanted to blindfold me, but always the diva, I wouldn't let them. They didn't insist; they left me on the bathroom floor and returned to the robbery I'd interrupted. It took me less than a minute to untie myself, and I considered going out and fighting some more. Common sense ultimately prevailed, and I waited until I heard them leave, locking me inside the apartment, before I emerged from the bathroom.

I ran to the balcony, almost tripping over one of the two bloodred metallic dining-room chairs en route, and started screaming: "Help! Help! I'm being robbed! They're coming back to kill me!" Luckily, some people were sunbathing on the roof of the apartment building below, and they called the police.

I surveyed the damage across the forty square meters, pacing back and forth past the frosted-glass partition that separated the living area from the sleeping quarter, while I waited for the cops to arrive. Afterwards, whenever I told this story, the first thing everyone asked was "What did they take?" as if I'd not only buried the lede but had forgotten it entirely, as if loss of material possessions somehow overrode potential loss of life on the scale of things most likely to cause post-traumatic stress and recurring nightmares.

But to answer the question, they took nearly everything of value, minus the furniture, leaving a mess of what they did leave behind. They stole my TV; my laptop (it was time for an upgrade anyway, as my friend Dave would point out a few days later, trying to inject a bit of gallows humor into what I was calling my near-death experience); my DVDs; my portable DVD player; a bedspread (?!); a wallet filled with cash, credit cards and my ATM card; and my cell phone (with the lawyer's phone number — so much for our hot date!). They let me keep my books (all in English, so of use only to the most highly literate South American robbers), my radio-cassette-DVD-player combo, and my iPod, which I'd refused to give up in the bathroom struggle, shoving it into the pocket of my track pants (diva strikes again!).

The cops arrived in what must have been five minutes or less, though it felt like a near-eternity. Through the peephole, I could see three of them slowly approaching the front door, guns drawn. They were able to enter the apartment because the robbers, tellingly, had left my keys in the lock — a sign that this may have been an inside job. It had possibly been arranged by people who had worked on the building while it was still under construction and therefore would have had keys to the entrance door, which, like nearly all apartment-building doors in BA, couldn't have been opened from the inside or outside without a key.

After the dust, and my head, cleared, I decided that a fourth partner had been hiding in the white van I'd noticed outside on my way into the building. (I'd assumed somebody was moving in.) He'd probably warned my three attackers that the owner of the apartment might be on his way up, which is why they had been waiting for me when the elevator door opened. But the lookout guy must have failed to provide them with a full description of me. In the aftermath of the robbery, once again thinking with rational clarity, I could have sworn the burglars looked slightly stunned that I wasn't a white *gringo* tourist.

   I had to do most of the detective work on my own. After their speedy arrival, the police were fairly useless. It didn't help that my Spanish was so basic, and only one of the cops spoke barely rudimentary English. I went with them in one of the two police cars parked in front of the building to the precinct's *comisería,* where I called my Spanish teacher Demian, who had been visiting his sister and her husband nearby. They all arrived at the station about fifteen minutes later to translate and provide emotional support, which was a lot more than the police offered. As would prove to be the case in all of my future experiences with them, they were more concerned with procedure and filling out forms than catching the bad guys. I could go on and on here about the cops in BA, but I'll get to them later.

   During the next few days, several people told me that pretty much everyone who lived in Buenos Aires had an experience like this at some point. During my decade and a half in New York, a city my dad never wanted me to move to because of its violent, dangerous reputation, I never thought it could happen to me. For the most part, I'd lived in doormen buildings, and that secure arrangement (annoyingly, at the expense of a considerable amount of privacy) had instilled in me a false sense of invincibility: Burglaries and robberies would always happen to other people, sometimes people I knew, but never to me. Now here in BA, I was being told that they were almost like rites of passage. The police didn't treat them like a big deal because to them, they weren't. Shockingly, some of my Argentine "friends" (now ex-friends) concurred and reacted in kind.

It was my first major learning experience in Argentina (with so many more to come — thankfully, none quite so violent). A woman who lived on the fourth floor, two stories down, also was robbed that day, but she was fortunate enough not to have arrived home in the middle of it. She told me that in a month, my life would be back to normal. I'd forget that it ever happened. I didn't see how that was possible, but I thanked her for her encouragement.

In the end, she was only half-right: My life did go back to normal, but I didn't forget any of it. I spent the next week in a rental apartment in Recoleta, a neighboring BA barrio, because I couldn't bear to return to the scene of the crime. Not yet. When I finally did five days later so that I could let the cops in to sweep the place for fingerprints — an exercise in ineptitude that probably should have been done on the day of the burglary — I had to go to the *parrilla* across the street and ask a young man who worked there to accompany me upstairs to my apartment. I wasn't convinced I wouldn't find danger once again lurking outside what had once been my domestic haven, and I wasn't taking any chances.

The psychological scars took longer to heal than my cuts and bruised ribs did. It probably didn't help my mental cause that I hung on to the bloodstained bandana/gag and the bloody gray *Brooklyn* hoodie that I had been wearing that day for months, without washing them. Once I got rid of all the forensic evidence, mental recovery finally was within my grasp.

The police never caught the criminals who had so violently invaded my personal space, which was hardly surprising, considering the lack of enthusiasm and the botched fingerprints sweep. And the face that the sketch artist at the police station drew the next day based on my description of one of the burglars, all of whom had appeared to be around my age (mid to late thirties), could have belonged to anyone. I must have seen it about a half dozen times in the weeks that followed!

Eventually, the face blended into crowds, fading from my line of vision, if not my memory, and I could tell people the story without flinching on the inside, and chuckle at my chutzpah. If anyone had asked me before that sunny Sunday afternoon in February how I would react in a robbery situation, I never in a zillion years would have predicted that I would actually fight back the way I did.

I learned a lot about myself and just as much about human behavior, who my real friends were, who my casual friends were, who my fair-weather friends were, and who just didn't give a damn. The latter list included Hernán, who brushed off my tale of woe when I relived it over a *locutorio* pay phone the next day, getting the facts of the case completely wrong because he was barely listening to them.

"You really need to be careful who you bring home," he admonished, with a hint of resentment that he was trying too hard to pass off as insouciance. The subtext was that I deserved what I got after rebuffing his romantic overtures on the dance floor. I felt like an assault victim who was casually being told that it was all my fault for encouraging predators with my sexy swagger and exposed Tag Heuer timepiece.

Who needed those so-called friends? I had learned so much about myself and the sturdy stuff of which I was made. I didn't need wingmen and bodyguards. I'd be all right, I kept telling myself. To ensure that I would be, I hardened my heart, swallowed my tears and resolved to protect my body and belongings at all cost.

Previously staunchly anti-gun, I considered exercising my right to bear arms before instead opting for an alarm system. I became harder, less trusting, something of an angry not-so-young man, ready to fight if someone crossed me (which would have made getting a gun a terrible idea indeed). Perhaps this me always had been lurking in the shadows, and it took being forced to fight for my life on a cold bathroom floor to bring him out.

It was a good thing I had someone stronger on my side, inside. I would need him to come to my defense again. It wasn't the last time my BA apartment would be a crime scene.

Don't You Know What The Night Can Do?

Your eyes are getting very heavy.

I wasn't reclining on an analyst's couch but rather, on my own, fading slowly, but more bored than sleepy. It was exactly how I used to feel as kid every Sunday morning between 11 and noon as I sat between mom and dad in the church pew, head nodding forward, eyes shutting, then suddenly reopening. It was as if God Himself was snapping an invisible rubber band in front of my face, playing some divine practical joke, or merely testing my reflexes.

What? I wasn't sleeping. I'm awake. I hope nobody saw that. Zzzzzz...

After an hour or so of open...shut...open...shut...open..., when the last "Amen" was finally said, my mind, body and soul always sprung magically back to life. It was my own weekly resurrection.

I hadn't been to church in years, so on that Sunday night in Buenos Aires, several weeks before the robbery, I couldn't blame my waning attention and listlessness on the preacher man. *Grey's Anatomy* wasn't doing it for me, so a little before midnight, I decided to get off the couch and go for a walk.

During my first year in Buenos Aires, I enjoyed few simple pleasures greater than strolling aimlessly through the streets between midnight and sunrise — as long as I avoided stepping into dog poo and ignored the glazed-eyed looks and drunken comments made by the occasional loitering *porteño*. (So *that's* how women feel when they walk past construction sites!) People would sometimes approach me and touch me as if they were trying to figure out whether I was African royalty, an American celebrity they didn't recognize, or just some freak of nature.

That was one of the social hazards of being a black man in a city where there were so few of them. Shortly after I moved to Buenos Aires, I met Hernán, who, at thirty-one, told me that he'd never even had a conversation with a black person until he met me.

"*En serio?!*"

"*En serio.*"

I still couldn't see how it was possible. It wasn't like he hadn't seen the world outside of Argentina. His boyfriend at the time was an American who was living in Washington D.C., a city with a significant black population, so presumably, Hernán had seen plenty of black people during his U.S. visits. But somehow, unfathomably, he had never talked to any of them.

I was his first, and in a way, he was mine, too — the first (and to date, only) man I ever devoured on the kitchen floor. That morning, the one that preceded my listless Sunday evening, we had gone back to my place post-Glam and finally gave in to our mutual lust. We did things I hadn't done before and didn't imagine I'd ever do on a floor. I knew I'd never look at that space in front of the stove the same way again!

After weeks of platonic friendship that began when Hernán complimented my pink Marc Jacobs shirt one night when I was on the back patio at Glam singing Kate Bush songs to my date Fernando (*"Wow! Wow! Wow! Wow! Wow! Wow! Ooh! Unbelieeeeevable!"*), we were finally ripping off each other's clothes. We never even made it to the bed, the same one I wasn't ready to crawl into some eighteen hours later.

As I hit the BA streets and inhaled the muggy summer air, memories from our long history — mine and BA's — came flooding back. I'd fallen for the Argentine capital during my first visit in April of 2005 while I was riding home in a taxi after dancing the night away in one of the city's many anything-goes-whether-you're-gay-or-straight discos. Something about the rising sun, the clear, blue sky, and the tree-lined streets rousing from their nocturnal slumber in the still of the morning made my heart skip a beat or two. I was drunk on love — and whiskey. Little did I know that this was the start of an up-and-down-and-up-and-down-again-and-again romance that would last longer than any of the ones I'd had with men.

None of my past loves and lusts could compare to Buenos Aires in the looks department. And that wasn't just because of the locals, many of whom were genetically blessed with the best physical features of two ethnic worlds: Hispanic and

Italian. In my next life, I wanted to come back as an Argentine, one with wealth, power, good looks and a kick-ass name, like Federico Pueyrredón.

The city, all tarnished glamor, like Gloria Swanson in *Sunset Boulevard*, was as stunning as a young William Holden, or any Federico I ever met there, and like all those handsome Federicos, its beauty was most apparent at night. Street lamps spotlit buildings and trees at various angles, creating a breathtaking and dramatic shadowy effect. During the day, I might have gotten a young mother with a boob hanging out, breastfeeding her baby on the ground next to a hot-dog vendor, or a couple sprawled out on the sidewalk, in the heat of heat, fast approaching the foreplay zone. Nobody seemed to notice because there were oddballs everywhere.

The freaks came out at night, too, but fewer of them were on display. Not having to maneuver through throngs crowding the sidewalks or couples nearly fucking on it, I was free to admire the retro architectural mix of functional and ornate. I couldn't get enough of those tall, slightly decaying buildings, which seemed to come straight out of some 1970s movie or TV show set in Metropolis, U.S.A. Riding in a taxi down Avenida Córdoba, from Avenida Callao toward Palermo, I half expected to see Mary Tyler Moore step out of one of the buildings and toss her hat into the air!

In spirit and sound, too, Buenos Aires was a city whose identity was defined by the past. Eighties music blared from car stereos and out of the transistor radios of street vendors (during my walk, I paused at a *kiosko* to enjoy a few bars of "Under Pressure" by Queen and David Bowie), and kids who were not yet born in that decade were obsessed with its greatest hits.

Even tango, Argentina's great musical and dance tradition, lived in the past, unabashedly and sentimentally reflecting on having loved and lost. Walking down Avenida Santa Fe that night, as on any given night, I was visited several times by that recurring sense of déjà vu that became a regular part of my life in BA. Looking into a store or a cafe, standing on a particular street corner, I would get the strangest feeling that I had been there before, in some other city, in some other lifetime, in some long-forgotten dream.

I'd been dreaming a lot — in and out of the bed I'd rejected twice that day. For me, Buenos Aires encouraged introspection and retrospection. It inspired anticipation and hope, too. It was the only city I'd been to other than New York where I woke up every morning with a feeling of potential and possibility: Anything could happen, and it usually did.

I felt grateful to be spending my late thirties there. It was a pivotal turning point in my life, a transitional period characterized by looking back and looking forward. I was old enough to have a wealth of memories and experiences to draw from but still young enough to have great dreams for the future. I felt like I was in the perfect place to try to make some of them come true.

    Three hours after embarking on my walk, I finally arrived back home, feet throbbing and body past the point of exhaustion. As my head hit the pillow, and I closed my eyes, I was already dreaming about the unexpected that tomorrow would no doubt bring.

My Baby's Got a Secret

It was Friday night in Buenos Aires, but I didn't feel like dancing. I just wanted to forget. I needed to erase every mental image of what had happened five days earlier and wipe away the trauma of being attacked and robbed in my apartment by a trio of burglars. It was such a brutal, stubborn memory, one in which I was forced to fight for life and limbs, three against one, on that cold bathroom floor.

At 3 a.m., when I sailed to Amerika, the one Buenos Aires disco where gays and straights had an equal chance of hooking up, I wasn't looking for a new world — just one with a little less Sturm und Drang. I was desperately seeking a distraction from my physical and emotional storm and stress. Cheap booze and a beautiful stranger might do.

Strapping and cocoa-skinned, with negative body fat and the sexiest tiny gap between his two front teeth, Lucas was just what I needed. He was easily the best-looking Argentine guy I'd seen across a crowded nightclub since moving to BA from New York City. I wasn't usually the one to make the first move, but on a night like this, whiskey brought out the sexy beast in me.

"*Hola. ¿Cómo estás?*"

He had me at "*Muy bien.*" One moment he was loitering by the balcony while I admired him from the bar. The next we were side by side, flirting, touching, squeezing. Although it was fun while it lasted, and I was tempted to try to prolong it at least until Saturday afternoon, at closing time, I got Lucas's phone number and left Amerika with my friends (but not Lucas) to go to Transformation, an after-hours tranny club.

Less than forty-eight hours later, we were on our first date, an Oscar party for two in the studio apartment I was renting for one week post-robbery in Recoleta, one barrio south of Palermo. Cuddling on a loveseat beside the bed, the fingers of my right hand and his left entwined, we watched together as *The Departed* won four Academy Awards, including Best Picture.

I was impressed by how many of the Hollywood actors Lucas knew, even if he hadn't seen any of the movies, and I loved that he seemed to get the classy-campy pomp of the proceedings. By the following week, he'd be handing out his own "Lucas Oscars" every Sunday morning while we were lounging in bed, the nominees being the five people, celebrity or civilian, who had said or done the most outrageous things during the previous week.

After the real Oscars, Lucas stayed over, but we didn't have sex that first night, nor did we do anything more than kiss. When he asked if it was OK if he took off his shirt to sleep, I thought it was refreshing — modesty in such a hunky package.

Within weeks, he and I officially were a couple. It was probably the most seamless — and rapid — transition from strangers to boyfriends I'd ever had, which raised at least one red flag. When I sent my best friend Lori an email telling her about Lucas, she was concerned. First, there was the huge age difference: I was thirty-seven; he was twenty-two. Had we both been ten years older, she reasoned, the fifteen-year gap would have been less problematic. But he was just a baby. "He was only one year old when Live Aid happened!" she marveled.

 Furthermore, I'd only recently had that life-altering and nearly life-ending experience on my bathroom floor. I'd recovered enough emotionally to return to my apartment and my regularly scheduled life, and my injuries were finally healing, but I was still having nightmares about the home invasion. In fact, the night that Lucas and I met, after I left him at Amerika and went to Transformation with my friends, I had a PTSD meltdown on the sidewalk that climaxed with me sobbing to my American friend Jeffrey on the phone as he rode in a taxi to the airport. I was terrified that the robbers would return to finish me off. Jeffrey was so concerned that he offered to cancel his trip to Uruguay, but I insisted that I'd be fine.

 Instead of going to see a therapist, I decided to fall in love. Lori thought it might be too soon to get seriously involved with someone, because I might be acting out of a need for comfort and safety.

 I should have listened to her instincts — or to my own. For weeks, Lucas and I didn't have sex. Although it bothered me, I was more suspicious than horny: I knew that gay twenty-two-year-old guys generally were not inclined toward abstinence or celibacy, and we were well past the point of taking things slowly.

One Sunday afternoon, after two months of intense makeout sessions and not much more, Lucas finally broached the subject we'd been avoiding for too long. The previous weekend we had gone away together to Colonia in Uruguay. The romantic trip hadn't changed our sexual status and had only made the elephant in the bedroom larger and harder to ignore. As we sat together in bed, Lucas explained why he was unable to have a normal sexual relationship. He said that he and his ex-boyfriend Carlos had broken up about a year and a half earlier, after Carlos raped him one night following an explosive argument about Carlos's infidelity. When Lucas threatened to go to the police, Carlos threatened him right back: If he told anyone what had happened, Carlos would out him to his parents.

Days later, Lucas went over to Carlos's house to confront him, and Carlos raped him again. As he offered this unexpected development in the story, several warning bells went off in my head. Had he been tested for HIV? (Yes, he had, he insisted.) And how was it possible for someone as big and solid as Lucas — six feet, two inches of pure muscle — to be raped by anyone? Apparently, the ex was even bigger and more solidly built.

Things with Lucas were never quite the same after he shared his story. We continued to date for another sexless month, and whenever we had a disagreement, he'd drag out the "I'm defective" card. "I don't work," he'd say over and over, as if that were a blanket excuse for every type of misbehavior.

I knew a major twist was coming, one that might have serious emotional consequences, but I wasn't ready to give up the security of our relationship. Despite our sexual shortcomings, Lucas was sweet and attentive. He understood my obsession with pop culture and even let himself get carried away with it, too. Also, because he was studying at university to be an English professor, I didn't have to struggle to communicate with him. He could help me with my Spanish homework and then go back to speaking English with me for the rest of the evening.

On the dark side, he was getting sick with *gripa* (the flu) all the time, and he'd never let me go with him to the doctor. Once he said his dad was taking him. Another time he said he hated going to appointments with an entourage. Something was not right, but I shoved my doubts aside. I wanted to delay waking up and living in reality.

I was forced out of my denial one Tuesday afternoon in late May. Lucas called me and told me he had something important to tell me in person. Immediately, I sensed it was going to be a matter of life and death. I didn't want to have to wait until that evening to hear what he was going to break to me — gently, I hoped.

"Tell me now," I pleaded.

"It has to be in person," he insisted.

That night he came over and told me that he had been to the doctor the previous week because of some blemishes on his back. The doctor ordered a series of blood tests and was alarmed by his low red blood cell count. That's when he suggested an HIV test. The results would be in on Friday morning.

Although I wasn't surprised, I still couldn't believe what I was hearing. Hadn't he been tested after what had happened with Carlos? He admitted that although he had been, he never picked up the results because he was afraid of what he might find out. So yes, it was possible that he indeed had contracted HIV from his ex.

That was when I had my first moment of clarity in months. Of course, he already knew that he was positive and probably had known when we met, which was why we never had sex and why he considered himself to be so defective. I wanted to blast him for not being up-front with me — who goes to the doctor because of such barely noticeable blemishes unless they're searching for something? — but he looked so sad and weak. Instead of confronting him, I tried to comfort him, focusing on best-case scenarios.

"A low red blood cell count could mean a lot of things," I announced while doing online research. "It could mean you're anemic. It doesn't have to mean you're HIV positive." I wasn't buying it, and I could tell he wasn't either.

Later, when we were going to sleep, he didn't take off his

shirt as he had the night of our first date, and every night after it. He left his jeans on, and his socks, too, falling asleep curled up in a ball on the edge of his side of the bed. It was almost as if he didn't want to risk infecting me by getting too close. When he left the next morning, his head hanging in shame, I knew it was over. I hoped I was wrong — about it being over, about *him* — but I was done living in denial.

On Friday, when he hadn't called me by 10:30 a.m., a half hour after he should have gotten the results of the HIV test, I prepared for the worst. About three hours later, it arrived via text message: "I'm sure that since you haven't heard from me until now, you know what the results were. . . ."

I didn't know how to respond. What was I supposed to say to the guy I suspected had been keeping such a big secret from me? Should I have scolded him? Should I have tried to offer some encouragement? I'm sure I settled for something closer to the latter, the trite politically correct equivalent of "I'm sorry for your loss." I *was* sorry — for my loss as much as for his. I knew we were over.

For the next several days, I went through the motions of my expat life. I went for hourlong runs around Palermo's parks and lakes, ordered delivery comfort food like *omelete con queso y papas fritas,* watched bad American TV on the Sony Channel while eating my cheese omelet and french fries, went out to all my local haunts (with the exception of Amerika — too painful) and drank way too much whiskey in single sittings.

Meanwhile, a dark cloud was perched over my head, which was usually bowed in defeat. At least I had one thing to be thankful for: Lucas and I hadn't had sex, so there was no pressing need for me to be tested for HIV. It wasn't the consolation prize I wanted, but thank God those sexless months ended up being good for something. The last thing I needed was to spend seventy-two hours wondering if I had it, too.

On one hand, I was relieved, and grateful that he'd considered my health. But on the other (the one I wanted to use to hit something — or someone, preferably Lucas), I was furious. Lucas may have spared me physically, but not emotionally. "How could he do this to me?" I asked myself over and over. I was even more certain that he had known he was positive all along, but the best way for him to avoid charges of deceiving me was to make it seem as if he had just found out himself. That was why he couldn't face me. I was angry about that, too. Didn't I deserve more than a stupid text message three hours after he supposedly found out? A phone call wouldn't have been nice, just appropriate.

He and I continued to talk sporadically via email for several weeks, but he seemed uninterested in everything, including me. I wasn't sure if he was trying to let go of me for my own good or for his own. One afternoon, I exploded in a fit of red-hot rage. I was fed up with our lack of real communication or face-to-face time (we hadn't seen each other since he'd left my apartment that Wednesday morning in total defeat) and his evasiveness about his situation and about us. Yes, *us*. Even with all of the secrets and lies of omission, this wasn't a deal-breaker, though it probably should have been. Not the HIV: those secrets and lies.

This wasn't, after all, my first brush with love and HIV. The night Lucas told me about his possible diagnosis, I told him about Miller, an ex-boyfriend I'd first dated thirteen years earlier who was HIV positive. He made his big out-of-the-blue reveal about a month into our year-and-a-half-long relationship, while we were sitting on the bed in my studio apartment on Avenue B in New York City's East Village, listening to Astrud Gilberto singing "How Insensitive" on the CD player.

"What a beautiful, sad song," I said, immersed in Gilberto's gorgeous gloom, though still inexperienced myself when it came to callous lovers.

"I know," Miller replied. "You know what else is sad? I have HIV, and there's nothing I can do about it." Just like that, he laid it on me.

At the time of Miller's HIV diagnosis in the early '90s, when he was just a few years older than Lucas was when I met him, it was tantamount to a death sentence. Miller responded by wallowing in self-destructive alcohol and drug abuse. He figured he was going to die young anyway, so why not live fast first? I spent more than a year watching what I was certain was a slow suicide from a front-row seat until one evening when Miller didn't show up at work or at my apartment afterwards because he'd been arrested for buying marijuana from an undercover cop in Washington Square Park. When I broke up with him over the phone the next day, I was pretty sure that if HIV didn't kill him, his recklessness would.

Miller survived, and although we still didn't work after we reconciled a decade later for a brief long-distance relationship — he was living in San Francisco at the time, I was still in New York City — it had nothing to do with HIV. Medical advances since the '90s had made both Miller's and Lucas's situation less dire, which was reflected in their reactions to it. Miller had given up drugs, alcohol and cigarettes, and was by then dedicated to living as long and healthily as possible. For Lucas, diagnosed more than ten years after Miller, the social stigma of HIV seemed to be a larger concern than his mortality. He worried that he was damaged, not necessarily doomed, goods. If his mortality was foremost in his mind, he never let on. But then, he didn't say much of anything to me after telling me that he was positive.

With all the anger that had been simmering inside of me finally boiling over, I sent him an email telling him how disappointed I was in him and his mishandling of the situation. I accused him of not only pushing me away unfairly but of failing to show any real concern for how his diagnosis might have been affecting me. I also admitted my suspicion — my certainty — that he had known all along. I didn't hold anything back.

He responded all full of self-righteousness and recrimination for what he saw as my lack of compassion, closing with the most passive-aggressive "I love you" ever, but he never denied anything. The email was so perfectly composed that I knew Lucas didn't write it alone. Although he was an English major, like many Argentines with near-fluency in English, his writing skills were somewhat clumsy. It infuriated me even more that the words he'd written to me weren't completely his own. Still, I resisted the urge to respond in kind, or at all.

For months, I was despondent. I lost myself for a little while trying to erase him from my memory by drinking too much whiskey and picking up strangers. One night when I was in Sitges, a gay pub near Amerika, sharing my sob story with a friend who was visiting from the U.S., he told me, "If you are looking for an apology, you might have to figure out how to go on without one." That's when I realized I had to let go — of my anger *and* of my ex.

By the end of summer, three months after I had last seen Lucas, my heart had mended enough for me to pick up the phone to call him. I wanted to *say* what I had to say, not write it, so there would be less risk of misinterpretation. He didn't answer, so I left him a message, apologizing for all the things I'd written in that final email and wishing him well. I didn't necessarily want to reopen the lines of communication between us, but I didn't want the last words he heard from me to be so full of hate and negativity.

He never called me back, but I did occasionally see him out after that. By the second or third time, we were no longer even acknowledging each other. The last time I saw him, he was with an older, overweight, sweaty-looking man at Sitges, and they were all over each other in the most ostentatiously sexual way, which was so unlike the Lucas I had dated for three months.

Although I was sitting with my friends right behind them, I was pretty sure Lucas didn't see me. He was blind without his glasses, which might have been why he was allowing himself to be publicly mauled by that particular guy. Maybe he felt he didn't have anything left to live for, so why hang on to his dignity?

But mine was perfectly intact. I didn't say or do anything. I just sat back and watched the show, relieved to be just a spectator and not one of the leads.

The Kick Inside

Marcelo had it coming.

Not only was he ruining my quality party time with Dave, who was visiting me in Buenos Aires from New York City, but Marcelo wouldn't take no for an answer. I could hardly see his eyes, which were obscured by long clumps of greasy black hair hanging from his scalp like malnourished black worms, and frankly, I didn't really want to.

For an hour after arriving at KM Zero, one of the trashiest gay clubs in all of BA but the only one to go to from Mondays to Wednesdays (which was technically Thursday morning), I hadn't been able to get him off of me. Every time I turned around, there he was, clinging and pleading, gyrating his lanky torso toward me like a serpent's tongue, leaning in for the kill.

"Un beso, por favor."

He'd grab me. I'd pull away. I explained that I just wanted to hang out with my friend, but he insisted on tagging along. I tried escaping to the bathroom to lose him. I flirted with better-looking guys. No matter where I went, what I did, he kept popping up right behind me, his hands and serpent's tongue everywhere I didn't want them to be.

Now, I was no prude. I'd gone out looking for fast love. I'd kissed, and I'd told. Yes, I'd been known to suffer fools and suffer from that after-midnight malady known as loose lips, especially after too many *whiscolas*.

But not that Thursday morning. Even had I not been with Dave, Marcelo wouldn't have had a chance. He was no Matías, nor Federico, nor Sebastián, all names that always seemed to be attached to irresistible smooth-operating Argentine males. I declined Marcelo's clumsy advances, turned him down flat. Again. And again. And yet again.

"I've already asked you nicely several times. Leave me alone. Get. The. Hell. Away. From. Me."

Snap! That's when he lost it. He grabbed the cup I was holding and spitefully spilled its contents — whiskey with a splash of Coke — all over the dirty, sticky floor and tried to flounce off in a huff.

That's when *I* lost it. I grabbed him to halt his escape, then retaliated with a shove and a swift kick in the shins, drastic actions for a guy like me, one who'd had his first real physical fight in decades eight months earlier, with three burglars on the floor of my apartment. I was pissed and pissed off. Was I the only single in the club? (Argentine men were some of the most gorgeous ones on earth, and after more than a year in Buenos Aires, I still couldn't quite understand what they saw in *me* when there were so many of *them* to go around.) Or did he think I owed him my attention simply because he was interested in me? So arrogant. So Argentine.

When I was through shutting him down, I glared at him and spoke slowly, for maximum condescending effect. "I'm going to the bar now. I can always buy another drink, but you can never buy class."

Ouch! I must have struck a nerve. I was pretty sure I saw smoke coming out of his ears as I walked away. He followed me and tried to convince the bartender not to serve me. No luck. I paid for my fresh whisky with a splash of Coke, sipped it and smiled triumphantly. Defeated, Marcelo curled his serpent's tongue back into his mouth and slithered away.

I thought that was the last I'd see of him. But about an hour later, Dave and I climbed the stairs leading up from the dungeon nightclub and went outside to look for an ATM. It was around 4 a.m., and Avenida Sante Fe, normally a madhouse of cars and bodies, was dark and silent. Only the streetlights broke the night with color, and the boarded-up storefronts seemed to be whispering "Shh!" as the chorus of Rihanna's "Don't Stop the Music" continued to pound in my head.

Before Dave and I even reached the Pueyrredón subway entrance right outside the front door, I saw Marcelo rushing toward us with a cop on either side of him. He was pointing and screeching at the top of his lungs, in Spanglish. "It's him! It's him! He's the one who did this! *Me dolio!*" He raised his jeans to reveal a huge scar on one of his legs. It was obviously a scabbed-over gash from some long-ago mishap, but he was crediting me with the handiwork. I couldn't make out everything he was saying, only that every other word was *nigger*!

It wouldn't be the last time an Argentine would go from

lusting to loathing in such a blatantly racist manner. Maybe it was the drugs talking — with the street lamp shining a spotlight on him, I could see clearly that he was out of his mind on something — but I was certain that his come-ons had been as racially motivated as his reaction to my rejection of him.

By then the club manager and one of the bartenders had come outside to see what was going on. The bartender spoke on my behalf. She told the cops that she'd seen the entire exchange, and I had clearly been provoked. To this day, I'm not sure how much she actually saw, but I was pretty certain that it wasn't the first time this particular patron had been embroiled in some sidewalk drama. I wondered if any of his other targets had been black like me.

It was out of the cops' hands. As I later found out, Argentine law compelled the police to investigate any complaint made by a citizen, whether he or she had proof or witnesses. That meant any random passerby who felt like ruining my day, or night, could have accused me of assault, or worse, for looking at them the wrong way — or simply for *looking* wrong. I would have to go with the police to the station.

"No way!" I announced. I wasn't going anywhere. This was a violation of my civil rights . . . my human rights. I felt like Martin Luther King Jr. (the sound of *nigger* was still ringing in my ears), or Norma Rae. Or the long-suffering heroine of a daytime soap. Why did it always have to rain on *my* parade in BA?

Dave pulled me aside and convinced me to cooperate. He would work the phones at the apartment, get in touch with the U.S. Embassy and try to find out what to do. Another friend, Atzin, a student from Mexico who happened to be passing by KM Zero on his way home from somewhere else at the peak of the commotion, offered to follow me in a taxi and translate at the station.

I reluctantly got into the backseat of the police car, uncuffed. The cops were treating me very nicely and respectfully, almost like a VIP. But I was furious. I had wanted to show my best friend a good time in Buenos Aires, and now the entire night had been sabotaged by some drugged-up horndog with a nasty racist streak. I was not amused.

My annoyance turned into full-on rage when we arrived at the police station, and one of the cops opened the back door for me and then had the gall to put his arm around me. He was only guiding me into the station, but how dare he?! For the second time that evening, my anger management went on break.

"Get off of me!" I shouted, pushing the cop away. He responded by grabbing me, wrestling me to the floor and cuffing me. As I kicked and screamed for him to let me go, he dragged me away to a cell. I only spent five minutes on the inside of the tiny box with bars, but it was long enough to convince me that I would never again end up in that situation

— until the next time some random fool decided to spoil my fun by accusing me of some imaginary crime.

Next, I was taken to the officer in charge, who ordered his underling to uncuff me and then went way off-topic by asking me to regale him with tales of everything I could remember about being in New York City on 9/11. WTF? *Now?* I wondered. After he took my fingerprints and my statement, he instructed a colleague to let me wait in a holding area of roughly sixty square meters, which was surrounded by small cells, one of which had briefly contained me a half hour earlier.

Did I want anything to drink or eat, coffee, a cigarette? So this was how Jennifer Lopez must have felt the night she spent handcuffed to a chair in the NYPD station on 36th Street (which happened to be right across from Dave's apartment in New York City) while cops asked for autographs. Considering that she and Puff Daddy were just innocent bystanders (or so they insisted) when members of their entourage began firing shots, she was a surprisingly good sport, by all accounts.

I, however, was not. I was angry and annoyed. Thankfully, Atzin was there to sedate me. He'd insisted on waiting with me in the holding area, and as a favor to their American guest, the cops allowed him to stay while the investigation was under way. I wasn't sure what constituted a BAPD "investigation," or why Marcelo never showed up for one that he had instigated, but for nearly five hours, I was locked inside the holding area, trying to figure out how a simple night out had turned into such a complicated disaster.

The waiting was the hardest part. During my time on the wrong side of door No. 1, the wooden one that separated me from the outside world (or, technically, the part of the police station that didn't require a key to exit), my mind occasionally wandered to all of the horror stories I'd heard about international jails. I kept thinking about *Brokedown Palace*. Wasn't that set somewhere in Asia, though? What a terrible movie. I surely didn't want to end up like Claire Danes in the end. For the second time since I'd moved to Buenos Aires, a chilling thought popped into my head: *What if I don't make it out of this alive?*

Yes, I may have been overreacting a bit. This wasn't exactly *Midnight Express*. At least there were a few distractions. About three and a half hours in, I was questioned about the earlier altercation with Marcelo (still MIA, as far as I knew) by an official-looking gentleman wearing a suit who also examined my arms and hands for bruises, and I was befriended by several on-duty cops who assured me that I had nothing to worry about. I also had an orchestra seat for a police lineup in which five young men had to step onto a platform and take off their shirts, while a middle-aged guy determined if one of them had committed some undisclosed offense against him.

Wasn't being in a police lineup humiliating enough without being forced to get half-undressed? I never did find out which one of the suspects — if any of them — committed that crime, but I felt a strange sense of relief. My skin color may have helped get me into my particular mess (I was still tossing around the idea of some sort of racist conspiracy, the sound of *nigger* only beginning to fade in my ears), and I'd probably be at the top of the suspect list for any serious crime committed by an unidentified black man in Buenos Aires, but at least in BA, chances were I'd never end being one of several look-alike guys required to remove their shirts in a police lineup.

Finally, around 9 a.m., someone came in and liberated me from captivity. I was a free man. That afternoon when I told my Spanish teacher about what had happened, Demian suggested that I look into pressing charges against the police department for wrongful detainment or something. I considered it, and even went so far as to consult an attorney (she sweetly and profusely apologized for the actions of her people as if they had been her own: *"Discúlpame, discúlpame"*), and I met with Gastón, an attorney and a representative from the U.S. Embassy whom Dave had contacted while I was behind bars.

Gastón told me that while the Buenos Aires police hadn't broken any laws by detaining me, they hadn't followed proper procedure, which was indeed a surprise development, considering what slaves to the bureaucratic process they usually were. First, the BAPD was prohibited from holding an American citizen without first contacting the

U.S. Embassy. Also, they hadn't allowed me to make my one phone call. Finally, it was a crime in Argentina to use racial slurs in public, a law Marcelo had broken every time he called me a nigger in front of the police, who hadn't done anything about it.

In the end, after some careful consideration, I decided to let it go. The case had been thrown out, and no long-term damage had been done. I considered leaving Buenos Aires, but Dave convinced me not to let Marcelo win. Eventually, my anger turned to amusement, and it became a funny anecdote to tell over drinks. The story, however, wasn't quite over.

A month later, I was heading upstairs at the nightclub Amerika, with Rihanna once again having her say, when I felt a clammy hand grab my arm.

"Hola, sexy."

I looked over. It couldn't be? Could it? No, no way. Yes way! It was Marcelo. This time he was even more persistent than he had been the first night. Obviously, he was out of his mind again, and obviously he didn't recognize me. After enduring several shameless entreaties from him, I spoke up, cool, calm and disgusted.

"You don't know who I am, do you?"

"No."

"Really? You don't recognize me?"

"No, do we know each other?"

"Because of you, one month ago, I spent five hours in a

police station."

Aha! It was like a lightbulb went off in his head. He looked mortified, though not because he hadn't recognized me. He began apologizing profusely. "I'm so sorry about that. I was really fucked up, and I didn't know what I was doing. Please forgive me."

"Did you even come down to the station that night?" I had to ask.

"No," he offered, softly and contritely. I was sure I saw a flicker of genuine shame in his bloodshot eyes.

He explained that he'd had a terrible altercation earlier that day with his ex-boyfriend, who was black, and he'd projected his ex's actions onto me. So this was his explanation/excuse? He was punishing me for the actions of that other black guy?

I wasn't surprised. Argentines liked to think of themselves as being unburdened by racism, but they were in denial. Although it was generally more silent than in the U.S., racism in Argentina was deeply entrenched and, in some ways, far more dangerous than when it was in your face and out in the open. After more than a year in Buenos Aires, I had learned that there was usually some racial motivation to any special treatment I received, positive or negative.

Appalled for ruining my night but not for his racist behavior (I didn't remind him how freely and publicly he'd used the *N*-word while ranting outside of KM Zero), Marcelo offered to go to the police station to tell the cops that it all had been his fault, and he'd lied to them about everything.

"That's OK. The case is closed." I'd had my fill of the BAPD, but unfortunately, the local police force would end up being major recurring players in my life over the course of the next few years.

"Let me know if you change your mind. I will do anything I can to make it up to you."

A moment of silence.

"So . . . will you go home with me?

I didn't answer him, but my laughter said everything I didn't have to.

Don't Talk to Strangers

I'd always considered myself lucky. During more than a decade of sexual liberation in New York City, I'd never picked up anything that was hazardous to my health because of it, nor had I lost anything of value.

That might be why I was caught so off-guard during my first trip to Rio in June of 2003, three years before I moved to South America. I'd heard all the travel horror stories about horny tourists getting duped, and occasionally killed, by rent boys and tricks in South America, but that sort of thing always seemed to happen to someone else, didn't it? That's exactly what I was thinking one balmy night when some locals I met in a restaurant on a dreary side street a few blocks off the beach invited me out after dinner and warned me to be extra-careful in the nightclub we were going to — in *any* nightclub in Rio!

The rules: 1) Order beer in a bottle, and don't pour it into a glass. 2) Don't accept drinks from strangers. 3) Keep cocktails covered with your palm or a napkin. You never know what someone might try to slip into your vodka tonic.

I hated it when people ruined all the fun with ominous warnings, but I did as I was told — that night. The following one, Wednesday, as I ventured out on my own into Rio's late-autumn nighttime air — stale, still and unseasonably steamy, dripping with humidity — I went back to my old reckless ways, accepting an invitation from the wrong man.

I'd met him on one of the streets that ran parallel to Copacabana beach, which, except for the occasional whoosh of the evening tide, was silent and deserted, a stark contrast to its daytime whir of activity and bronzed heavenly bodies in motion against a blue-on-blue backdrop, inspiring devilish mental tangents when you were trying to focus on sunblocking *your* torso. I was asking a cop for directions to a bar I'd read about in my Frommer's travel guide, and the guy, who'd overheard, offered to walk me there.

"Can I join you inside?" he asked after we'd walked in silence through several lonely-looking blocks to get there.

"Sure." I answered, happy to have the company. As he went off to buy us drinks, I thought about last night's travel advisory. He was handsome and neatly pressed. He seemed like a pretty decent fellow. He hadn't set off my gaydar, so I assumed he was straight, which meant that he probably wasn't expecting anything sexual in return. I didn't even consider that he might be after the fifty dollars in Brazilian *reais* that I'd just withdrawn from the ATM. I'd paid our cover charge, but the first round of drinks were on him. He must have had his own money.

We ended up going to a few other watering holes and finally to one of the beachfront beer stands that was pretty much the only weekday sign of nightlife on the water. By then, the situation was getting blurrier and blurrier, and so were the black sky and the waves approaching from the horizon. I figured the beer had just gone to my head more quickly than usual, but I was too out of it to analyze my level of inebriation. The last thing I remember were the words of a concerned bartender who whispered something in my ear after my drinking buddy excused himself to pee on the beach: "Be careful. He's going to rob you."

And then I woke up — more than twenty-four hours later! I wasn't sure if the bartender was imaginary or real, but he had been right. When I arose from my long slumber, I was facedown in bed in my five-star suite at the Sofitel, fully clothed. The room was a mess, and it was spinning, too. I tried to stand up, but my feet gave out. I went back to bed and passed out for a few more hours.

When I woke up again, I tried to put together what had transpired. I looked at the clock on the nightstand. It was 10 a.m. on Friday morning. What had happened to Thursday? Had I slept through the entire thing? I began to have flashbacks. I remembered stumbling through the lobby, coming upstairs in the elevator, a back rub, and then nothing.

By then I knew I had been drugged. I surveyed the damage. Some robbery! He had taken one credit card, my cash (which by then had amounted to about twenty-five dollars), a bottle of Dolce & Gabbana cologne and my deodorant. I wasn't sure why he wanted my deodorant, but at least I'd picked up a crook who was big on personal hygiene. That had to count for something. I was less upset about what he had taken (not my camera, not my iPod and, thank God, not my passport) than by the fact that I'd lost an entire day in Rio!

I stumbled downstairs to the business center. I sent an email to Lori to tell her what had happened, and I received one from Kevin, the guy I was dating in New York at the time. He was dumping me. I'd sensed something was off for a while. He hadn't contacted me since I'd left New York, and I noticed he had been strangely distant in the days leading up to my departure. One of the last things I'd done before going out on Wednesday was send him an email asking him what was going on.

In his reply, he wrote that he had planned on waiting until I got back from my 10-day getaway, then something about how we weren't a match, how he wanted a T-shirt—and-jeans type of guy who spent hours working on his car (a strange aspiration indeed, coming from a thirty-two-year-old man who called Deee-Lite his all-time favorite band). I responded with all the clarity I could muster in my shaky state, keeping my reply short but not so sweet. I blasted him for leading me on for months. Surely he'd known I wasn't what he wanted from the moment he first saw me. (It wouldn't be until I moved to Buenos Aires that I'd discover T-shirts and jeans, and if I'd had a car to work on, I would have paid someone else to do it.)

I told him that I'd been robbed, though not that I'd been drugged beforehand. I was still trying to process that part, and frankly, I was too embarrassed — over being dumped by Kevin before I could dump him and over being duped by a stranger in Rio — to get into it. I wanted to compound his guilt with as little damage to my ego as possible. Hurt and furious as I was, though, my rage would have to wait. I had to deal with more pressing matters.

I called Alexandre and Ana, a Brazilian Will and Grace I had met when I was in São Paolo the previous weekend and with whom I'd hung out a few times in Rio. They came over, comforted me with hugs and encouraging words about how it could happen to anyone, and took me to file a police report at a nearby cop shop. They also let me cry on their shoulders over being dumped by Kevin on what already was one of the worst mornings/early afternoons of my life.

After Ana left to go to work, Alexandre stayed behind and kissed some of the pain away. Before meeting up with them later that evening, I had a good bawling session on the phone with Lori. I could have dealt with losing Kevin, or being dumped for the first time, or having my first holiday disaster, or losing my faith in the decency of sweet-talking pickups, or missing an entire day of my vacation. But all of them in one fell swoop of misfortune? Too much.

You'd think I would have given up on men after being screwed over by two of them in one day, but I didn't. The great thing about LoiSuites Recoleta, the five-star hotel where I stayed during three holidays in Buenos Aires, the first of which was two years after Rio, was that the front desk required visitors to present identification before going up to the guest quarters. This was for the protection of the hotel's clientele. If anything went missing, the culprit would be easier to find. It was also a good way to find out the name of the person you were about to bring upstairs!

Once I moved into my doorman-free building in BA and no longer had a vigilante front desk looking out for me, I was on my own. Occasionally I'd bring the wrong guy home, pass out and, like Amy Winehouse in one of her most devastatingly haunting songs, I'd wake up alone. I lost some things over the course of several petty thefts — house keys, a little cash, a few articles of clothing, a digital camera, a laptop — but never my life.

I guess I should have considered myself still lucky. Actually, I did until one night about two years after I moved to BA when I brought home one particular stray waif who stuck around until the sun came up. By the end of the morning, I'd be sorry he did.

I couldn't remember his name or the exact circumstances under which we met. I did recall being with him on the dance floor at KM Zero, drunken conversation by the bar, and bits and pieces of the taxi ride back to my place. After I woke up and looked over at the diminutive smooth-skinned stranger in bed next to me, studying the twelve o'clock shadow on his face, I wondered if I should search his clothing for identification. What was his name? How old was he? *Who* was he? I was just about to reach for his trousers when he began stirring and crawled on top of me. He gave me a blow job, and then fell on his back and stared at the ceiling.

"Cómo estás?" I asked, figuring it was as good a morning-

after opening line as any.

"Bien. Cansado. Y vos?"

"Bien." I paused awkwardly while coming up with the reason why he had to leave. *"Tengo que preparme para almorzar con un amigo."*

What a lie. I didn't have to get ready for a lunch date with a friend. It was just my way of saying, "It's been nice, but it's time for you to go." No, it wasn't my best moment, but from the stories friends had told me over the years of their adventures in hosting and being hosted by pickups, I knew there were far more insensitive ways to tell a trick to hit the freeway.

He looked disappointed. He got out of bed and slowly got dressed. As I watched him, my impatience turned into anxiety. I wondered if time, or this guy, could possibly move any more slowly. I wanted him *out*. Once he'd tied the laces on his running shoes, he stood up and looked at me.

"Te cobro doscientos pesos."

"You've got to be joking," I said in English. "I'm not giving you two hundred pesos!" I'm not sure if he understood the words, but he got their meaning. He insisted that we had agreed on a rate before we'd left the club the night before, and now payment — roughly sixty dollars — was due.

I may not have recalled every single detail of our conversation the night before, but I knew that no matter how much I'd had to drink, I never would agree to pay for sex. I had a theory: He had woken up, seen a few nice things hanging around and figured he'd take advantage of the stupid American and pose as a "taxi boy," Argentine slang for those sweet young things — some gay, more straight — who trolled bars and clubs offering sexual favors for pesos.

The only problem was that he was picking on the wrong American, one who had been swindled by too many Argentines and knew every trick in the unwritten book *How to Fuck Over Visiting Gringos*. I'd tangled and tangoed with a few taxi boys in my time but never for money. "Pay you?" I always asked, insulted that they'd approached me. "You should be paying *me*!" They never did, but a few of them (Martin, Ismael, Leo, who never actually admitted to being one, though everybody knew better) always waived their fee with me.

The guy and I had a bit of back-and-forth. "I don't owe you anything," I said. *"Págame!"* he insisted. Rinse. Repeat. Under the harsh, unforgiving spotlight of the pre-afternoon sun blazing brightly through the blinds (and without booze goggles to impair my vision), his large, protruding eyes, beaklike profile and spindly frame made him look like an oversize bug. If only I could squash him like an insect and go about my day. I considered picking him up and tossing him over the balcony. That way, I'd get rid of both the scrawny body and the bill.

It wasn't the money, though. I easily could have given it to him and bid him *chau*. Had this happened during my early months in BA, I would have done just that. But I was fed up with *porteños* and their inclination to try to rip me off. He wasn't getting a single peso from me. I just had to get him out without resorting to violence.

I looked at the hooker/thief sitting on the couch, staring at me, refusing to budge. I was surprised by how calm he was, polite almost, except for the fact that he was trying to take advantage of me. Part of me wished that he would break something, get violent, so that I would have the perfect excuse to respond with force.

After ten minutes of stalemate, I called the police, who arrived quickly. I went downstairs to let them in, while my neighbor's houseguest, who (along with Rumi, the wife of Maxi, my building's *portero*) was privy by then to all the sordid details of my dilemma, kept an eye on my apartment and the unwelcome guest inside of it. One of the two cops asked for a recap of the action, and the bug told them that we had arranged a meeting on a rent-boy website, and I had agreed to pay for services to be rendered. I was less shocked by the lie than by the fact that he was outing himself as a prostitute to the police. Wasn't prostitution illegal in Buenos Aires?

I handed over my Hewlett-Packard laptop to the cops and told them to search my browser history. They'd find no evidence that I'd visited such a website. This was simply a case of my picking up someone who decided the morning after that he'd try to score in and out of bed.

The police explained that although prostitution was illegal

in Argentina, if we had made an agreement that I would pay him, I would have had to honor it. In this case, however, there was no proof, so I was acting within my rights when I demanded that he leave.

The con artist, however, wasn't going down so easily. Still refusing to go, he hurled threats at me, making a motion with his hands as if he were slitting his throat. When he finally did leave, it was in handcuffs. Prostitution may not have been a punishable offense on that particular day, but making threats in front of the police was. One of the cops warned me to be more careful when letting people I didn't know into my apartment. Not everyone in the bars and clubs can be trusted. He said it completely without judgment, as if he'd said it countless times before.

I took his advice seriously and resolved to tighten up my guest list. Though I'd continue talking to strangers and occasionally taking them home, resulting in a few more petty thefts, this would be the last time the cops would have to make a house call on my account. I accompanied them downstairs with their detainee, relieved to be done with this particular drama and relieved that, for once, the BAPD actually got something right.

This House Is Empty Now

"hola jeremy soy maxi encargago en tu edificio llama a la persona que alquila tu departamento por que robaron en tu departamento hoy a las 17 hs"

Uh-oh, here we go again *again*!

Thus began my latest inner monologue after receiving Maxi's Facebook email, thankfully, from the relative physical and emotional safety of Bangkok, the capital city I'd landed in four months after my March 2011 departure from Buenos Aires, launching a seventeen-month on-off love affair/semi-residency. My mind was racing, each thought tumbling toward some uncertain conclusion that would remain just out of reach. . . .

Another robbery in Buenos Aires, and more breaking bad news on Facebook. If *you* didn't hear it first (or see it first, firsthand), chances are you heard it first on Facebook, or Twitter, both of which do a better job of quickly getting stories into circulation among the general population than network news programs or any major-city daily newspaper these days. They're where the majority of the news that's fit to print — and some that isn't — seems to go right before it spreads to the masses. If I'm ever diagnosed with some serious medical condition, it's possible that I will read all about my prognosis in my Facebook News Feed before my doctor has had a chance to deliver the news to me in person.

As unwanted social-network notifications go, the Facebook

message that I received one Saturday afternoon in April of 2012 from Maxi, the *portero* of my Buenos Aires apartment building, was right down there with mass invitations to events in cities on continents where I don't live, all of those BranchOut emails, full-length movies in Flixster and Hidden Chronicles requests. Lower even.

Newsflash! My apartment was robbed again. It would be like déjà vu except, unlike the break-in more than five years earlier, I didn't come home from lunch to find three men lurking outside my front door, waiting to pounce on me — but only because I was two relocations removed from Argentina, in Thailand, where I'd first landed in July of 2011, following four months in Melbourne.

God knows I should have been accustomed to receiving news that might ruin my morning, or the entire day, week or months (as would be the case on this occasion), on Facebook. It was the place where I found out that Farrah Fawcett, Patrick Swayze, Elizabeth Taylor, Amy Winehouse and three of the four Golden Girls had died, and where I realized the full devastation of Hurricane Sandy, via the status updates and pictorial posts of my friends in the New York City tri-state area. But grim celebrity and meteorological updates are nothing compared to when the story is all about you.

On the bright side, better that it happen in 2012 than ten years earlier. Back then, when I'd run off to London and/or Europe on vacation twice a year, I was far more isolated from everyone back home: Emails could take days to be received and responded to, and my mobile-service carrier never seemed to have a plan that allowed me to make international calls at a reasonable rate. In the '90s, before everyone had personal email accounts and laptops, mini-notebooks, iPads and iPhones to constantly check, it was worse. I used to call my editors at *People* magazine collect back then from non-cordless hotel phones in order to make sure there were no outstanding questions on any of my stories.

By 2012, I was pretty sure that people didn't even make collect calls anymore. A few months after the robbery sequel, when my mother told me that her job as manager of the communications department at the Hyatt Regency Atlanta was being eliminated, I was sorry for her impending loss, especially since she'd been with the company for nearly forty years, but I also wondered what had taken them so long. She said that she and her staff of switchboard operators eventually would be replaced by computers, but with Facebook, Skype and all those other apps people were always talking about that I hadn't gotten around to trying keeping people connected on opposite sides of the world, wasn't functioning Wi-Fi throughout the hotel all that was really necessary?

The wireless connection in my Bangkok pad allowed Maxi to be the bearer of bad news on Facebook only hours after it happened. Assuming that Maxi had been dealing directly with the BAPD, I responded to his message, asking him to contact Bri, the woman who was managing my Buenos Aires apartment, which I had been renting out to people on holiday in BA, or to have the police do so. Some help *he* turned out to be: He didn't write me back until the following Thursday. I wondered if he'd lost his Wi-Fi signal.

Later in the evening, after one round of emails with Bri, I spoke to her live via a computer-to—cell phone conversation on Skype that literally cost me pennies. It was the first time I'd heard her voice since I hired her to look after my place and handle check-ins and checkouts the day before I left BA for Melbourne, some fourteen months earlier.

She said that two other apartments in the building had been broken into on Friday, but the police were not allowing her to enter my unit to survey the damage because she did not have written authorization giving her power of attorney over my apartment affairs. It was an oversight that I'd considered once or twice in the previous fourteen months without guessing that it would come back to haunt me in that particular way.

I was sure scores of rental apartments in Buenos Aires were being robbed every quarter. If the renters were lucky enough not to be home at the time, did the police bar them from entering until they could present an official lease or the owner's bill of sale? What if I had entrusted my apartment to a friend rent- and lease-free? Would he or she have been locked out of it for weeks — *months* — while I negotiated BA's legal bureaucracy with Bri, multiple lawyers, the U.S. embassies in BA and Bangkok, and my friend Mariem, an Argentine law student who, thanks to my dilemma, received a crash course in BA real-estate law? The rules that were presumably put in place to protect me were beginning to feel more like a punishment.

Lost rental income and getting Bri a U.S. government—notarized letter granting her power of attorney and then persuading a judge to approve it so she could once again have access to my apartment weren't my only concerns in the nearly seven months before I regained control of my BA real-estate investment. I was worried about the police, too. I hadn't had the best experiences with them in BA, and I knew they couldn't be trusted. Bri later explained to me that they often were in cahoots with burglars and *porteros* to rip off as many Buenos Aires homeowners as possible. But poor me: Repeat robberies like mine were practically unheard of. And now the dirty cops, the same ones who would later offer Bri entry into the apartment for a fee, had uncontested and unlimited access to my former abode. What if they took whatever the intruders had left behind?

And furthermore, why such on-the-job diligence by the BAPD one home invasion too late? It had been a long weekend in Buenos Aires, and as Bri explained, that meant burglars were more likely to strike because so many people were out of town. Of course, if many of the cops were in on the crimes, then it was open season for them, too. Luckily, the last renters had checked out two days earlier, so my apartment was unoccupied during the break-in, unlike the first time. I imagined they were sad to leave BA, but in doing so when they did, they'd dodged two bullets: robbery *and* homelessness!

While we stumbled through those kilometers of bureaucratic red tape, trying to secure the appropriate authorization for Bri to enter *my* apartment, I was, for the most part, surprisingly calm, which was either the influence of Buddha, or the fact that there wasn't much in my BA apartment to steal. Unless the robbers arrived with a moving crew to haul away the furniture, the most they got away with was probably the television set (a cheap, old-fashioned model — not even flat-screen — that I didn't exactly splurge on, having anticipated this exact scenario after losing a far more expensive brand in the great robbery of 2007), a coffeemaker and a printer/scanner.

But as with the first time, it wasn't what they took or didn't take. It was that old feeling of being violated by intruders. The only difference was that during burglary No. 2, I didn't have to fight off three of them on the bathroom floor. For once, I was in the right place at the right time.

And speaking of timing, on that fateful morning when Maxi broke the bad news on Facebook, my birthday was one week and two days away. Less than twenty-four hours earlier, possibly at the very moment of the break-in, as I was thinking back on my festive birthdays in BA, I was on the verge of becoming slightly homesick.

By the time I blew out the candles that evening at the Metropolitan Bangkok, where Lori, who was visiting me from New York, threw an impromptu pre-birthday celebration for two, my nostalgic mood had passed. From then on, I would just feel annoyed every time I thought about BA, and grateful that I was anywhere but there. Nothing cures homesickness quite like an expensive reminder of one of the main reasons why you left town in the first place.

II. Contemplating Color

I Never Picked Cotton

"There's a thin line between love and hate."

When The Persuaders sang those words in the 1971 pop classic of the same name, they were really on to something. There is, apparently, also a thin line between fetishism and outright racism, being eroticized for being exotic and being stigmatized for the same reason.

Aside from the loss of any semblance of anonymity, my biggest frustration with being a gay black man from the U.S. in South America (and, later, in Australia and Southeast Asia — or any place where we are a rarity, not just a minority) was that from the moment many people saw me, they dragged out and dusted off those ancient stereotypes about black men, sizing me up the way I assumed they did all the others who seldom crossed their paths. Everyone wanted to know the same thing: "Is it true what they say about black men?" I heard that question over and over on three different continents, coming from countless people who had seen few black men in real life but assumed they already knew the answer.

Sex for the first time with anyone began to feel almost like an audition, especially when I was sober enough to take it all in. Size mattered when you were black in Buenos Aires (or Melbourne, or Bangkok, all home at some point after I left New York City): Either you fulfilled the fantasy about the big black dick, or you probably wouldn't get a call back. It was such a deflating process that a couple of years into my life in BA, for the first time ever, getting hard and staying that way became, well, twice as hard. The rules: The top, which all black men were generally assumed to be, did all the heavy lifting and thrusting. The bottom just needed to lie there, waiting to take it in, all eight or more inches of it.

Being someone given to underperforming under pressure, I was always nervous at auditions — and not just the ones I was sent on by that talent scout who stopped me one morning on Avenida Santa Fe after my Pilates class. Once I was familiar with the lay of the gay land in Buenos Aires, aware of just what they saw in me and what they expected to see *attached* to me, I became wary of practically every suitor I met, just waiting for them to screw up by mentioning my skin color, or asking that dreaded question: "Is it true what they say about black men?"

Still, I sometimes had a hard time saying no (not just to the question but to the guys in general), and over the course of two weeks of conversation on MSN Messenger, I deflected Alvaro's amorous advances without declining them outright. He didn't impress me much when we first "met" on Gaydar, the first gay dating and hookup website that I ever used (our version of Match.com, but with more cocks and ass — even Boy George supposedly had a profile!), and he went on and on about how much he loved black men, how his last boyfriend was black, blah blah blah.

Bleh!

Before going off on his boring black tangent, he asked if he could say something without offending me. I gathered that Alvaro, like so many other *porteños* in Buenos Aires who prefaced those tangents similarly, must have suspected that no black guy actually wanted to hear about a white guy's insatiable appetite for chocolate. So why did they still insist on going there? Even less appealing was the general aura of desperation about Alvaro. In short, I wasn't feeling him.

Whenever he sent me an instant message, if I bothered to respond, it was usually a monosyllabic reply, cordial but with minimal enthusiasm. I ignored his Facebook friend request, too. Undaunted, he continued to pursue me on a daily basis. Finally, one day, exhausted from sparing his feelings, I decided to level with him. I told him as bluntly and succinctly as possible that I just wasn't interested in going out with him. *Ni ahora, ni nunca!*

Now, I was accustomed to the poor manner in which *porteños* generally reacted to rejection. They were hot, then they were cold, and they could go from charming to vicious mid-sentence. But this previously mild-mannered guy's response stunned me nonetheless. It was way over-the-top, even in a country where melodrama was always the fresh catch of the day, served up hot and spicy.

"sos un negro de mierda que se cree que eres muy importante para hacerte el dificil, tendrias que estar recolectando algodon en Alabama, imbécil! Go home, fucking yankee nigger!"

I could read him getting angrier with each passing word, even dropping in some cotton-picking slave imagery for poetic effect. Perhaps he included that final sentence because, let's face it, racial bigotry is so much more powerful in English. It pretty much summed up the spirit of the rest. Intriguingly and disturbingly, his message, vile though it may have been, was the only time I found him even remotely interesting. But I would have taken boring over racist every day of the week.

Alvaro's words made me wonder what was lurking just under the surface of some of those white guys who were so obsessed with black men. Argentines liked to think of themselves as not being racist, but I knew better. After all, the country, the whitest in all of South America and proud of it, shipped off its black population to the front lines during the wars of the nineteenth century, essentially using them as human cannons as part of a crusade to whitewash and Europeanize the country.

For all the historical and deeply entrenched racism in Argentina, in some ways, as a black man, I had it better there than my ex-boyfriend Lucas, an Argentine whose dark skin tone created for him its own set of poor social conditions. The paucity of black people in Argentina meant there was no need to organize any unofficial movement against them. There weren't enough of us to bother. And whatever Argentines considered my social status to be, on a sexual level, I'd never been more desirable. Black men were seen as exotic and erotic, a must-do before you die.

When Argentines basked in their own superiority, hoisting themselves up on a self-constructed pedestal, they usually seemed to be looking down on their darker fellow countrymen and on the more ethnic-looking citizens of other South American countries like Bolivia and Peru. As the South American country with the largest European-descended populace, Argentina has a significant number of natural blondes and people with blue and green eyes. A visiting friend once commented that if she were walking down the street in Buenos Aires and had no idea where she was, she easily could have made the mistake of thinking she was somewhere in Europe, or even the U.S.

The more European-looking Argentines used their whiteness to their advantage, creating a sort of caste system based on skin tone, much like the one instituted on U.S. plantations during the slavery era and still largely in place within the U.S. black community. This hyperawareness of skin tone was even built into their language, with *negro* (Spanish for "black") being used interchangeably with *morocho* and *moreno,* as an adjective and a noun, to endearingly refer to both black people like me and dark-skinned Argentines.

Lucas, though good-looking and highly desirable by any standards outside of Argentina, was a *morocho* who'd spent most of his childhood in his pale big brother's white shadow. Family, friends and strangers saw to it that he entered adulthood with a solid inferiority complex for being a few shades too dark. The same people who treated him like a lesser person because he was off-white treated me like a black superstar, though for reasons that were mostly sexual.

Light versus dark became a recurring theme in all the great cities I called home after leaving the U.S. in 2006. In Australia, it took the more familiar (from a lifetime spent living in the U.S.) form of white versus black, with the lighter ruling class saving most of its discrimination for its own "black" people, indigenous Australian Aborigines, as well as Asians, Arabs and "wogs" (Aussie slang for people of Mediterranean descent).

I was shocked every time I read another front-page news story about some white Australian footy star using a racial slur against a fellow player, not because of what was said, but because the epithets almost always seemed to be leveled at someone of Middle Eastern or North African descent whom most Americans might consider to be Caucasian or "white." As an American black man, I didn't have to worry about being called names or being the butt of racist jokes. I was an exotic stud, superior, in a sense, to white Americans, whom many Australians I encountered considered to have no redeeming qualities. At least I was probably great in bed!

The light versus dark hang-ups of Thais were more similar to those of the *porteños* in Buenos Aires, with darker skin seen by many as being inferior to lighter. I saw women on the streets of Bangkok dolled up in Kabuki-style cosmetic masks, and in Boots pharmacies and local supermarkets and beauty stores, you could buy whitening creams and face cleansers because if you were Asian, the products seemed to say, you could never be too light-skinned. The locals in Southeast Asia often complimented me on the color of my skin, but for many, "black is beautiful" didn't seem to apply to their own kind. The more European (i.e., white) your skin tone, the better.

The majority of overt racism I encountered in Asia, from locals as well as Western tourists, was anti-Asian, not anti-black. Gay Thai men as well as Asian and Western tourists were surprisingly comfortable specifying "No Asians" in their Grindr and Manhunt online-dating/hooking-up profiles. "Whites only" was tantamount to "No Asians," judging from the number of people with "Whites only" in their profiles who came on to me.

In my seventeen months in Southeast Asia (and in all my time living outside of the U.S.), I never came across one person with the guts to put "No blacks" or "Not into black guys" in his dating profile. I wasn't sure if this was because there were too few of us to bother doing so, or if it was because the U.S. was the only place where gay white men were comfortable being so casually and publicly racist against gay black men.

I was sure Thai people harbored their share of racist attitudes against black people, but as in Argentina, it was neither systematic nor organized, and its sexual undercurrents were much stronger than the social ones. I never got the sense that Thai people thought of me as being inferior because I was black. Aside from the novelty factor, I never got the sense that Thai people thought about me much at all. Though darker than everyone around me, I was, for the most part, merely the size of my penis there, and to some, preferable among black men because I was American and not African.

The complicated but more subtle forms of white-on-black (as in African-descended) racism I noticed abroad resulted in my feeling more comfortable in my own skin tone than I ever did in the U.S., where people were far more likely to wear bigotry on their sleeves. Not that I wasn't profoundly affected by racial profiling in South America, Australia and Southeast Asia, but I never "suffered" under it the way I had in the U.S. My skin color influenced how people abroad thought of me sexually, but I never got the sense that they were forming any other meaningful opinions — particularly negative ones — about me based on it, the way so many white people did in the U.S. That's why I was ill-prepared for Alvaro's sudden outburst and found it so shocking.

It wasn't a first, though, and it wouldn't be the last time that an Argentine suitor would turn on me like that. They never seemed to take rejection well. I suspected that had I been white, Alvaro would have backed down amicably. But how dare I, a fucking Yankee nigger, so inferior to him in every way, turn *him* down? A similar thought must go through the mind of a rapist who takes what he wants when it's not given to him willingly. I still didn't quite know what to make of the Argentine racist. There were so many parallels to the Southern plantation owners who used to regularly bed the slaves they whipped and looked so far down on.

Alvaro probably would have been one of them — only forcing the male slaves to bend over to his will. I was thankful to be living in a time when I could decline a white guy's advances and only suffer verbal abuse as a consequence. Unfortunately, many women still didn't have that luxury. Alvaro likely forgot all about me in a week, and went on trolling the Internet, trying to sleep with people he actually despised. I couldn't think of a more fitting life sentence.

Skin I'm In

In the days after my encounter with Alvaro, still smarting from his racist outburst on MSN Messenger, I sought mental solace in the more soothing prose of James Baldwin, Zora Neale Hurston and Toni Morrison, black writers whose words had changed my life at various points in it. Unlike Baby Suggs — the mother-in-law of Sethe, the heroine of Morrison's classic novel *Beloved* — who spent her final days in bed contemplating color ("Took her a long time to finish with blue, then yellow, then green. She was well into pink when she died"), my focus was black and white and the shades of gray that represented universal attitudes about the polar-opposite hues.

In search of some objective perspective, I posed the following question on Facebook: "Have you ever used the *N*-word? And if not, could extreme anger ever drive you to use it?"

The responses ran the gamut, but the honesty of one, in particular, from a former classmate at Osceola High School in Kissimmee, Florida, surprised me, for both its candor and its cluelessness:

"Let's face it; you know people are going to lie about this answer!!! I, on the other hand, have said it! And no, it is not because I am prejudiced. I haven't ever directly said it to someone's face either, but whoever was with me at the time has heard it come out of my mouth."

Uh-*huh*.

In other words, if you would dare to use the word *nigger* but not directly to the person it's intended to demean, you might be a coward but not necessarily a racist? Was that what she was saying? Really? How Paula Deen of her.

And how deluded, I thought, and dissented emphatically — though in the interest of not starting a Facebook war, I resisted the urge to call her as I saw her: She was a classic closet bigot. Calling a black person a nigger in the privacy of all-white company or even in your own mind is just as racist as shouting it from the rooftop of a slave plantation.

To use the word *nigger* in reference to a black person (especially in anger and outside of the hip-hop *nigga* context), whether in private or in public, to someone's face or behind his or her back, even to think it, means that you harbor racism within. To some degree, you consider black people to be inferior to white people. Contrary to popular belief, you don't have to wear a white sheet with a pointy hat and go around burning crosses to be racist. I believe that nearly everyone, myself included, to some minute degree or more, is prejudiced — if not against blacks, against some other group. We all harbor prejudices of some kind, and many people are carelessly and casually racist while being perfectly pleasant otherwise.

Several of my Facebook friends reasoned that when people are angry, blinded by fury, they are driven to hurt the person responsible for their rage in the worst way possible. Fair enough. I couldn't argue with that. Still, it was a weak defense that would never hold up in the court of politically correct public opinion. Anger is never a justifiable excuse for violence, nor is it one for racist speech.

No matter how many black people you sleep with, how many you date or how many friends you have who are black, to use the word *nigger* as a nonblack person is to directly express and reflect the negative way in which you regard black people. (To those who carp about black people calling each other *nigger* in jest, I say, I don't love it, and it sets a poor example, but no matter how you try to spin it, due to the word's historical context and representation of oppression of blacks by whites, it's simply not the same.) Sure, there may be varying degrees of bigotry, from passive and racist mostly in thought to confrontational and violent, but in the end, it all comes down to the same thing.

That's also true with pejorative expressions based on sexual preference. Years ago, during an argument with my brother Alexi, who is also gay, my sister, Janine called him a faggot. Though she probably never gave it a second thought after she'd cooled down (just as Alvaro likely forgot all about his own "nigger" tirade — until his next one), it was seared into my memory. From that moment on, I was never able to look at my big sister without hearing her hurling that epithet at my brother and wondering what she really thought of me. I never forgave her for it, and our relationship went up and down before steadily deteriorating into nothing at all.

I haven't spoken to her since December of 2005.

Months after my last telephone conversation with my sister, my other big brother, Jeff, the straight one, dropped the *F*-bomb on me during an argument by email. "You're a stupid faggot that nobody likes," he wrote, in response to my leveling the *L*-word (*loser*) at him. I never spoke to him again. I bring up my fractured sibling relationships because, as I see it, racism and homophobia are two sides of the same coin. I can no more bring myself to have a relationship with someone who'd call me a faggot than with someone who'd call me a nigger.

I once read a *New York* magazine article that quoted John Amaechi, a former NBA center who is both black and gay, expressing a similar opinion regarding the separate-but-equal status of the two words in the chain of insults: "As a black man, there is no difference between calling me the *N*-word or calling me the *F*-word. Both words make me want to kill you."

In a sense, *faggot* can be even more hurtful because gay people haven't co-opted it as a term of endearment the way rappers and some blacks have done with *nigger,* draining the word of some of its venom. *Faggot* suggests homophobia as much as *nigger* coming from a nonblack does racism, and I find homophobia and racism equally unacceptable.

I've often found that racism is particularly strong in the male gay community, which is disappointing because, of all people, they should know better. We spend our youths feeling like outsiders, and our adult lives clamoring for equal rights, all the while excluding people and cherry-picking based on skin color and ethnic background, then blithely defending it with the *P*-word (*preference*).

I never did much online dating when I lived in the United States, but my friend Rob, who is also black and lived in Buenos Aires at the same time as I did, told me about how hyperselective some single white guys in the U.S. were in their online-dating profiles. "No blacks" was a popular demand, and "Please be white" was chief among their criteria.

"Please be white"? I'd rather be asked about my penis size than read something like that. To me, it's only slightly less aggressively racist than "No niggers allowed." But like the former schoolmate who responded to my Facebook query, these choosey lovers probably wouldn't describe themselves as prejudiced. They'd explain it away with a tossed off "Sorry, that's just my preference." Why not leave race out of it and simply ignore the messages you receive from black guys as you would messages from white guys whom you don't find attractive? "No blacks" and "Please be white" exclude and demean, and they come across as hostile, all qualities that are at the root of racism.

And what about people who respond to those profiles? Are they racist by association? I think to a degree, yes. Why would a nonracist person give a second glance to someone who has a "whites only" rule when it comes to dating? Yes, I understand that, like the heart, the dick wants what the dick wants. But as soon as you write the words "Whites only," you have completely dismissed entire groups of people. And that is what prejudice, discrimination and racism are all about.

Unfortunately, as proven by Alvaro, who was so casually racist in his response to my rejection, the "whites only" folks aren't the only enemy. Those who fetishize blacks are just as likely to harbor dangerous levels of racism. Because, when you get right down to it, fetishizing blacks indicates an overawareness of race that is a main ingredient of racism. Even the term coined to describe it — "jungle fever" — is offensive, suggesting that black people are wild and untamed, feral animals, and to be attracted to them is a sickness.

Rob told me more disturbing stuff about an ex-girlfriend who was white. When he broke up with her, she responded with venom: "I should have known this would happen if I dated a nigger."

We are sleeping with our enemies, I thought as Rob shared his story. It made me suspicious of everyone who crossed my path. No, we never know what people are really thinking, which makes life both interesting and terrifying. I've been dumped before. I cried. I threw things. I lashed out. I entertained dangerous thoughts. I got angry. But I never resorted to name-calling.

In the end, the response of Rob's ex-girlfriend, of Alvaro,

of everyone who dares to utter, or think, the *N*-word while chasing black guys online or in clubs has nothing to do with me. If you've been sleeping with trash, or *trying* to sleep with trash — and that, basically, sums up how any nonblack person who uses that word views black people — what does that make you?

You're White, Dance Like an Enemy!

As part of my study of the dating and mating rituals of gay men around the world, I created a profile on Manhunt Australia a week into my relocation from Buenos Aires to Melbourne, after about a year and a half off the online meat market. Though it would be more than a month before I'd meet any of the guys who messaged me (an honor that went to Nathan: tall, blond and handsome, with a predilection for giving blow jobs on deserted Melbourne back streets), hearing them out cleared up what I admit may have been a rose-colored view of the typical Aussie male.

Yes, he was still more ruggedly handsome, more charming, taller than his counterparts just about everywhere (those photos and screen images of Hugh Jackman, Eric Bana and all of the hunky Aussie up-and-comers crowding the Hollywood scene didn't lie), but they weren't necessarily as flawless as I may have made them out to be in my mind when I was in Oz as a visitor.

In fact, they were only human. They had warts and all, and they, too, were cursed by one of the most shameful of all human character defects: racism. While I never actually witnessed any blatant acts of bigotry in my day-to-day offline life in Melbourne, my first two weeks of Manhunt messages taught me that while the primary targets may change, racism lurks in every corner of the world.

Exhibit A:

Hey mate, You are hot! Anymore pics?

Flattered, I checked out his profile to see what he had to say. At first, I was impressed. He was good-looking, and he seemed to have a decent enough grasp of language ("anymore" for "any more" notwithstanding, but I was accustomed to imperfect grammar and spelling after spending four and a half years being surrounded by people who spoke and wrote badly broken English in Buenos Aires). Unfortunately, in offering all of the pertinent details about himself, he saved the worst for last:

Only interested in Caucasian guys between 25 and 45.

I cringed but decided to take the bait, so I responded.

Thanks, buddy. But I'm not Caucasian!

His response did nothing to reverse the negative impression he'd already made. In fact, I was even more turned off.

I can see that! lol! For some reason I get a lot of Asians messaging me, that was for them!

His words got me thinking: Was what he was saying really so bad? We all have our preferences, be it for a certain height, a certain hair color, a certain body type and, for some, even a certain religion. We accept all of that, so why should skin color be exempt?

Is a white person wanting to be with another white person any worse than a black person wanting to be with another black person, an Asian wanting to be with an Asian, a Latino wanting to be with a Latino? Does that make them all racist?

Was I just being overly sensitive after watching the ladies on *The View* spend two days debating the implications of Donald Trump's demand that U.S. President Barack Obama release his birth certificate for public inspection?

Here's what the Oxford English Dictionary had to say:

PREJUDICE: Preconceived opinion not based on reason or actual experience; bias, partiality; (now) spec. unreasoned dislike, hostility, or antagonism towards, or discrimination against, a race, sex, or other class of people.

RACIST: An advocate or supporter of racism; a person whose words or actions display racial prejudice or discrimination. Also in extended use: a person who is prejudiced against people of other nationalities.

With all due respect to Oxford's lexicographers, the way I see it, it's not quite so simple. Prejudice is not necessarily racism. Prejudice in relationship to race is more about blindly and stubbornly embracing stereotypes and hanging on to preconceived notions about ethnic groups. It emphasizes attitude and thoughts more than actions and personal philosophy. One can harbor isolated prejudices about black men, especially ones that aren't necessarily negative — assuming they're all good basketball players, or that they've all got big dicks, sight unseen — without being racist.

Meanwhile, racism is more systematic and deeply ingrained. It involves an inability or unwillingness to look past personal prejudice, stemming from convictions about a racial hierarchy and the superiority of one's own race, and leads to discrimination, ostracism and, far too frequently, violence. While most of us would acknowledge harboring some degree of prejudice, we tend to see racism as the province of extremists like skinheads, neo-Nazis and the Ku Klux Klan. But racism need not be so angry and theatrical. There are scores of casual racists among us who would never raise a hand to a black person or call one the *N*-word.

Those who are so unyielding in their racial preference that they'd take the time to include it in their Manhunt profile, specifically to discourage a particular race from contacting them, have crossed over from prejudice into the realm of racism. This person was discriminating against an entire group of people (Asians) presumably based on the way they look or act, as if they all look or act one particular way. His blasé attitude and response, the way he almost seemed to be inviting me into his circle of bigotry (note the You-know-what-I-mean? exclamation mark), indicated that he didn't even realize how dangerous his attitude was, which made it even more so.

Someone explained to me that the large number of Asians living and working in Australia, a majority minority that had surprised me when I first visited Oz some six months earlier, led to racism targeted specifically at them. Aborigines, commonly referred to by Aussies as "black" people, bore the brunt of their bigotry, too. For once, my shade of "black" was off the color hook.

But getting back to sexual preferences, no matter how hard you try to make the apples-and-oranges comparisons work, skin color and ethnicity are different from hair color or height or body type. Yes, being disqualified romantically because of how tall you are, how thin you are or the hue of your hair hurts, but deadly wars have been fought, crusades have been launched, people have suffered and continue to suffer around the world because of racially motivated genocide and ethnic cleansing. Race and ethnicity aren't things that you can change with a trip to the hairdresser or a few months with a personal trainer. Like being gay (if you buy the nature over nurture argument), you're born that way, and you stay that way.

Appealing to "Caucasians only" in your Manhunt profile is not just about the type of man you want to fuck. It sends out a message that it's OK to disregard entire ethnic groups and casually advertise it online. Attention, so-called chocolate queens who are "interested in black men only": That means you, too! To those who say, "I can't control what I like," racial preference isn't nearly as ingrained as sexual preference, and it's far less black and white (no pun intended). An open mind leads to an open heart. Gravitating toward one race or ethnicity doesn't have to mean completely dismissing another, especially so publicly and so off-handedly.

That guy's whites-only dating policy was nothing compared to the laundry list of dating and sexual no-nos in the profile of this other man who messaged me. Let's call him Bigot_in_Au. He didn't even try to bury his racism, opting to lead with it instead:

IF ANY OF THESE DESCRIBE U YOUR NOT FOR ME THANKS!!

*Asian

*oldies

*do not offer me money

*dont be way hairy/over weight

*dont be queeny

*dont just be out to get laid

*most important DONT be up yourself

Well, he got his points across (in the most badly spelled and poorly punctuated way), and I'm sure all of the Asian men left him alone, but I suspect so did all of the decent white ones (and this black one), because on Manhunt, or anywhere you happen to be looking for the perfect male, racism and a nasty attitude are even uglier than love handles.

Do You Wanna Touch Me?

My crash course in Australian racism wasn't the only lesson I learned on Manhunt. Within 24 hours of posting my profile — the one with six photos revealing nothing below the belt — I made a few other discoveries: 1) An Aussie acquaintance I'd met in Buenos Aires a couple of years earlier had left BA and returned to Melbourne to study. 2) Gay men in Australia were even more comfortable with online nudity than the ones in Argentina. 3) The art of the perfect come-on wasn't lost only on Argentines.

Oh, and 4) A dog in heat will write just about anything to get splashed!

After a while, all the dirty talk started to blend into one giant bag of trash. Of course, it wasn't all lust and lewdness around there; some of the messages were polite and actually kind of sweet. But the more colorful ones made me wonder how many seemingly perfect gentlemen who we meet through normal offline channels were privately talking shit online. It was something to think about the next time a gorgeous guy on the subway/tram/bus/sidewalk wearing an expensive designer suit caught my eye.

Warning! The 10 most entertaining Manhunt messages I received over the course of that first day are not for the prudish. Some are kind of graphic. Nausea might ensue, then laughter:

10. *ever free wed nights or thursday mornings?*

Thursday mornings? I was tempted to respond just to find out what, or who, had him so tied up the rest of the week.

9. *Fuck me*

Short, not so sweet, and straight to the point. Sometimes, though, less is, well, just less.

8. *how big is that cock of yours?*

Ah, penis size: a recurring theme Down Under, too! It wasn't just an Argentine obsession. Perhaps I was under that impression because I'd never done the online thing until I moved to Buenos Aires. Maybe it's just the way of the gay online world.

7. *yum u should charge to let ppl blow u ;)*

Something to consider if the job search didn't work out?

6. *Hey dude how's it going. You look really hot ;-) I'm coming to Melb for a holiday in may and am looking for any black guys that are interested in meeting. I've never been with a black guy b4 so would love to meet someone. I'm a bttm and I'm friendly and chilled. Anyway dude let me know if you're interested. No stress if you're not. I thought it was worth a try lol Cheers ;-)*

Ah, the dreaded chocolate virgin! A word of advice to any who might be reading this: If you're hoping to introduce chocolate into your sexual diet, keep it to yourself. You'll increase your chances of sweet success.

5. *I'm guessing ur not interested..apparently I'm the worlds best deepthroater.....not to mention a great fuck ;) But thats cool if I'm not ur thing I'm not ur thing..thats life*

eh. I love to please hot tops, I'm obsessed with black dudes, not indian, nothing else, african all the way. let me know if you change ur mind, take it easy

I had to give this one credit for being persistent. I never responded to his messages, but he kept trying, and although he lost his cool (if he ever had any), he never lost his temper, which his Argentine equivalent probably would have done after the third ignored plea.

4. *Would love 2 suck your cock sometime. If interested,let me know. xx*

Got it.

3. *damn honey, you are sooooo damn fine :) experience raging bottom here :)*

"Raging bottom" not only sounded unappealing but kind of unhealthy, too.

2. *hows things.. hot profile and pics there :) where in melb are you? would love to lie back and watch yr body as yr pumping me sometime... looks hot as. interested, let me know. cheers*

Just what I'd been looking for: a lazy bottom who can't spell.

1. *hey man last black dude i was with had a hugely thick dick.. couild barely get it in.. is that common??*

Stop! In the name of love! It was the man of my dreams!

Though I hoped I had only just begun to scratch the surface of things I'll see and do in this lifetime, one day into Part 3 of my Project Manhunt Australia — a.k.a. The Cairns

Experiment, following similar test runs in Melbourne (Part 1) and Sydney (Part 2) — I was convinced that the written word couldn't possibly get any more hysterical than it was when it came straight from the keyboard of the horny and black-curious.

Someone pointed out to me that people tend to write things from the anonymous safety of behind their computers that they'd never dare utter in real life. I'd certainly concur, but I'd take it one step further by saying that this might very well be when they show you who they really are.

In Sydney, with a few exceptions, I found the guys to be as polite online as I would have expected them to be had they been seeing me for the first time in person. They were still persistent, but their commentary was sane and sound, neither offensive nor particularly quotable, which, in the case of Tomas, a 36-year-old Irish expat living in Sydney who had the best bedside manner I'd experienced since leaving New York, worked in his favor.

The manhunters were once again completely unfiltered when I got to Cairns, more than likely to hand over their phone numbers to a complete stranger online! I spent most of my time on Manhunt there with my jaw at keyboard level while reading my messages. One memorable threesome:

1. *Hey mate, please take this as a compliment, "you look lik the fuck of a century" Correct me if im wrong but i reckon you would know how to do a tight ass like it should be done*

2) *hi hows your night going, what you upto?? Mate you have got such a cute smile and your very good looking, your body is amazing and so horny, I bet you have a big cock, Ive never seen a guy like you naked before what a dream.*

3) *hey sexc man, il be in cairns wed nite. U wana play n hav a good session, i crumble 4 dark guys so u cn make me ur slave 2 do wot eva u wish. Send me a text.*

My Manhunt adventures in Argentina and Australia left me fully prepared for Bangkok, where kids said — and wrote — the darndest things, too. Yes, *kids*. So many of the Bangkok locals, expats and vacationers I encountered on PlanetRomeo, ground zero for online dating in the Thai capital, acted like boys, the barely postpubescent variety that was just discovering sex for the first time.

A few offered to pay me for my company. One expat from L.A. knew where I lived, when I worked out (thanks to his room with a view of my hotel's gym) and how many movies I watched every night (via my public Facebook status updates), while I didn't even know what he looked like. Creepy, yes, but kind of intriguing, too — though not enough to make me actually want to meet him. At least nothing he said was as predictable as the myriad messages I got from horny "bottoms" desperately seeking a "top" and others wanting to know if it was true what they say about black men.

bottomseektopinbkk: *love u be my forst black dick fuck me*

i am 39 german

Me: *I don't think so.*

bottomseektopinbkk: *no problem then fuck someone else blacky*

Unfortunately, even if had I wanted to, my options weren't exactly charming my pants off:

i really love african man...im malaysian malay..i really love african man..im a boy...im NOT a girl.. i really looking for african boyfriend. i wnt to feel african dick in my mouth and ass.. i like free african man... if u really wish to fuck my ass plz contact me with this email or add me on yahoo messenger;... ..do u interested?

Not tonight. Not *any* night.

American Idiots

In nearly 20 cumulative years of traveling and living abroad, I don't believe I encountered as much anti-American sentiment as I might have overheard during one hour spent eavesdropping on locals — or talking to just one of them — in an Australian bar. Considering how ravenously their country devoured American pop culture, Aussies had surprisingly little tolerance for what they perceived as the American way.

I was at BNH Hospital in Bangkok with Rudie, an Australian friend on holiday who was having a setback in his recovery from a motorcycle accident months earlier. He was checking out against doctors' orders, having spent two days in a private four-star room there receiving regular injections of morphine to ease the chronic pain caused by a torn ligament in his left shoulder. We were in the waiting area filling out paperwork when a young lady from Los Angeles approached the counter and began talking in English to the nurse on duty about how she volunteers at a hospital back home. Rudie stopped writing, turned around and glared at her. You would have thought that she, and not I, had caused his re-injury after pulling his arm too hard while dragging him to the dance floor at DJ Station several nights earlier.

"I hate Americans," he sniffed. "Why do they always have to talk so loud? If you're sitting in a room with several conversations going on, the only people you ever hear are the

Americans."

Never mind that he was talking louder than anyone in *that* room, or that he had just finished berating the staff, loudly, for not being attentive enough during his stay, or that he was talking to an American. Perhaps he figured that since I hadn't lived there in nearly six years, I didn't count. Or that since I was born in the U.S. Virgin Islands, and Caribbean culture had been as much of an influence on me growing up in Kissimmee, Florida, as mainland U.S. culture had been, I didn't count. But how would he have known where I was born, and how it had made me different from your typical Yankee? He'd never bothered to ask, and like so many people I'd met in Australia, there was no digging beneath blanket stereotypes when it came to anyone who fit into any cultural or ethnic box (Asians, Aborigines, Americans).

At least they didn't hate black people. Although I noticed as much of an awareness of color in Australia as I did in South America and Southeast Asia, Australians were less obvious about it. Sure I'd get that dreaded question from time to time — "Is it true what they say about black men?" — but the majority of the gay guys I encountered in Melbourne were savvy enough to know that if they were rude enough to ask, they weren't likely to find out.

If only they were equally savvy when it came to the topic of Americans, whom so many Aussies seemed to dismiss out of hand: They were fat. They were greedy capitalists. They didn't travel, and they didn't speak a second language (which would have given them at least one thing in common with nearly every Australian I knew). They were rude, racist, loud and they had terrible taste — in clothing, in food, in politicians. Worst (possibly) of all, they were gun-wielding maniacs who had sacrificed their morality for the right to bear arms.

One night I was talking to Dov, a fellow American in Melbourne (a Bostonian who considered himself a New Yorker because he'd spent his last few years in the U.S. living as one), and he had very few nice things to say about the folks we'd both left behind. I wasn't surprised. Most of my expat American friends in Argentina were not particularly fond of non-expat Americans either, and to be perfectly honest, I probably still wouldn't have been living abroad if I didn't harbor my own anti-American sentiments.

But we all have our flaws, I'd discovered. Four and a half years living in Buenos Aires magnified the shortcomings of Argentines to such a blinding degree that I sometimes had to look away. And after four months in Australia, I could see clearly now that Aussies were not without their own not-so-appealing regularities. When I returned to Melbourne after six months in Southeast Asia, one of the most beautiful, fascinating and culturally rich areas on earth, and all everyone seemed to want to know was whether I'd done any trekking, I thought it nicely summed up everything that's shallow about some Australians, as if seeing them drunkenly stumbling around bars in Phuket and Bangkok in their

Havaiana flip-flops hadn't been revelatory enough.

What irked me most about all of the negative American stereotypes — aside from the fact that they often were upheld by people who had never set foot in the U.S. and got all of their information from the media and prime-time TV — was that the same folks who spent so much time damning Americans also embraced American television, flocked to American movies, obsessed over Hollywood celebrities and dreamed of one day making it big in the USA. Sure, it would mean toiling in the modern-day equivalent of Sodom and Gomorrah, but it was still nice work if you could get it in America.

That must have been one recurring thought running through the mind of Russell Watson, the British tenor who, for years, tried to make it in the U.S., with some degree of success. One day I was reading an interview with him in Melbourne's Sunday *Herald Sun,* and he was talking about being diagnosed with a brain tumor twice, in 2005 and 2007. Of course, he received the first diagnosis in — where else? — the USA.

"It was my worst fears confirmed. I was in L.A., and it was like a scene out of *ER*. I went to an office where an American man in a white coat said: 'Mr. Watson, please sit down.' I felt like I was back at school in the headmaster's office. It was all very American and dramatic in the way it was presented. 'Mr. Watson, you have a brain tumor and from the images we're getting, I'd say it is a big one.' There was a sense of 'Oh.'"

"It was all very American and dramatic in the way it was presented"? "Very American" because it was presented so dramatically and not with that typically British detachment? American hospital dramas were always giving us these images of stoic, stone-faced doctors doling out bad news with only slightly more emotion than U.S. government workers swatting away pesky customers at the Department of Motor Vehicles. "Don't get emotionally attached," I'd heard them say over and over amongst themselves.

Had *Grey's Anatomy* and *Private Practice* gotten it all wrong? Maybe there actually was a lot of hand-wringing, desperate looks and, occasionally, even tears. They'd all seem fitting to me: Being told you have a brain tumor, as a family member of mine was in 2011, is a dramatic experience deserving of a dramatic presentation. Was that being "American" or simply being human? The most baffling part of Watson's trip down memory lane was not his doctor's bedside manner but that "sense of 'Oh.'"

Oh. Maybe he was referring to the formality, the this-is-a-very-important-moment-please-cue-somber-music approach. In Argentina, I often was disarmed by the inappropriately casual manner of medical workers. *"Tranquilo,"* they'd say to me when I unleashed my inner hypochondriac and assumed the worst possible diagnosis every time I went in because of some minor ache or pain or blood-test result that didn't fall into the optimal range. Of course, I never received bad news from any of my doctors in BA (and, in reality, I never actually expected to), so I had no idea how they adjusted their tone to deliver it.

I wondered how it was done in England. "Oh. By the way, you have a brain tumor. Would you like another cup of the tea?" I was hoping that the writer would get Watson to clarify his "It was all very American" comment, which I interpreted as being unnecessarily pejorative, as well as that sense of "Oh," but his name was Nui Te Koha. God only knows what *he* thought of Americans!

You Can Get With This, Or You Can Get With That

"I don't find Asian men attractive."

I didn't say it. He did: EJ, the European expat who had been living in Bangkok for 10 years. For some reason, he wanted to know if I was attracted to Asian men (my answer: when I found them attractive), and although some things would have been better left unsaid, he felt the need to tell me that he is not.

My first instinct was to ask why he would live in a country where he wasn't attracted to the people, but I'd already met his longtime partner, so I figured that hooking up with the locals wasn't a priority.

My second instinct was to ask him what exactly he found attractive, then. His boyfriend? If I had lined up every man in the room and arranged them from the ones I found most attractive down to the least, starting at the bar, his boyfriend might have ended up somewhere near the bathroom. It wasn't the nicest thought that ran through my head that evening, but that was just my taste.

This was exactly EJ's response when I suggested that his attitude reeked of racism. Like most men with the no-Asians dating and fucking policies, EJ hid behind the old "That's just my preference" excuse. He compared his not being attracted to Asians to his preferring men over women. I let that one slide because it was such a ridiculous argument. It was as misguided as equating it to digging brunettes over blondes. Both rationalizations were irrelevant. All sexual preferences are not created equal, and for EJ to so glibly simplify human sexuality just for the sake of his weak defense against my charge of racism just made him seem deluded times two.

But if we are going to assign labels to what EJ considered to be preferences, regardless of what determines a person's sexuality (nature vs. nurture), there is already a term in use for guys who prefer men to women — a word as objectionable for many as being called "racist." And if there were a catchy term to describe blond-chasers, I would have coined it. "Racist" is the operative word to describe someone who would exclude someone from housing, from jobs, from sex, from love, based on ethnicity. Furthermore, no matter how people want to spin it, rejection for being a certain race stings so much more than being overlooked because of your hair or eye color, or even your gender.

When I carefully considered EJ's words, though, I had to give him a little credit. He hadn't said, "I would never date or sleep with an Asian guy" (though I'm sure he would have, had I probed). He'd simply made a blanket statement regarding sexual attraction based on race, which was in the same neighborhood but on a different street. EJ seemed like a smart, decent person, and I gave him extra credit for getting the reference when I mentioned EJ DiMera on *Days of Our*

Lives. I certainly hadn't meant to offend him when I called his attitude racist any more than he'd meant to annoy me when he expressed said attitude, but the battle lines had been drawn.

He wasn't entirely unsuccessful in his attempt to defend himself. He did make me think that perhaps I should cut him and all of the others who had made similar comments over the previous few months some slack. Though I wasn't going to back down from my accusations of racism, I didn't really see them as the enemy, not the way I had my two redneck classmates at Denn John Middle School in Kissimmee, Florida, who used to chant, "I smell nigger," every time they passed by me.

I didn't know enough about EJ to measure the degree of his personal prejudice on a scale from one to ten, but I knew he was walking through life — and DJ Station — seeing groups and types rather than individuals. In his outright dismissal of Asian men, he was forming a sexual hierarchy based on race, while basically saying that all Asian men are created physically equal with little variation: "A few undesirable physical qualities fit all. I'll put the entire Asian population in a box and remove them from my dating and sexing pool."

Never mind that eye shape aside, there's actually little physical similarity among the men of, say, Thailand, China and the Philippines, and even less among those of Israel, Lebanon, India and Anatolian Turkey (all of which are part of the Asian continent, making their natives just as Asian as the ones to whom EJ was referring). Shoving them into one box of physical attributes and labeling it *Do not touch* is tantamount to saying that all black people look alike. Sure we have no control over what we're attracted to, but we can control whether we see people as individuals or merely as belonging to groups that are determined by ethnicity and race. And does rigid adherence in your head to a supposed "preference" (which, as expressed, often sounds more like a rule: "I don't date [insert ethnicity, race or nationality here]") become almost self-fulfilling in practice, to the point of exclusion?

The highly evolved modern man thinks outside of boxes and beyond ethnicities, not limiting himself to what he prefers. There's a difference between liking one thing more than another, and dismissing either of them out of hand. "I am not attracted to Asian men," like "I don't like broccoli," is less a statement of preference than one of taste. People's tastes, like their preferences, aren't necessarily static, as anyone who grew up hating ice cream (or broccoli) but likes it as an adult knows. Isn't that the whole point behind an "acquired taste"?

If you can't, or won't, think outside of boxes and beyond ethnicities, at least be courageous enough to face the uncomfortable implications of your color vision. "Jeremy, I think I might be racist.... I'm just not attracted to Asian men," a German friend in Berlin once confided in me, earning my respect, if not a free pass. "Sorry, I just don't find them attractive," with no interest in self-reflection to determine why, is a cop-out.

Before I met EJ, I would have imagined that someone who had been living in Asia for a decade would have realized that the contents of the Asian box are as varied as those of the white, black or Latino ones. But EJ and people just like him were too busy using their "preferences" as an excuse to exclude an entire continent of people from the list of guys they would sleep with to see the variety among Asian men.

I'd become accustomed to that attitude in Australia. In fact, I'd come to expect it. I'd anticipated more enlightenment when I came to Southeast Asia on an extended holiday after four months living in Melbourne, but it was actually worse, with Asian-on-Asian racism being as rampant as black-on-black racism in the United States (and European/white Argentine vs. South American/brown Argentine racism in Buenos Aires) and highlighting the social ill in bright shocking pink. I told EJ that I found comments like his particularly offensive because I'd spent most of my life hearing similar sentiments in the United States, only they were usually aimed at black men there.

This form of non-gender-related sexual discrimination against the locals in Asia felt equally inappropriate, perhaps more so: They were being insulted by visitors in their own home. I couldn't condone "Whites only" (i.e., "No Asians") in Australia, but I understood that some of it came from a territorial place. It was partly the manifestation of resentment of a minority that was growing larger every year. But there is no excuse for relocating to a country to benefit from it economically (or for whatever personal reason), descending upon the gay scene, and then basically saying you don't like the way the locals there look.

En masse, it sometimes felt like small-scale colonialism, with the European male in the position of sexual power — everybody wanted *him*. As I watched the division of ethnicities at DJ Station (Asians on the ground floor, Europeans on top) and listened to people like EJ constantly voicing the racial limits of their attraction, I wondered what the future might hold in an increasingly mobile, diverse and app-obsessed gay world. With Grindr and SCRUFF overtaking bars and clubs in boy-meets-boy preeminence, would virtual "walls" of segregation and apartheid (*Edit Filter*) one day replace velvet ropes as the No. 1 way to keep out the undesired?

Hadn't history taught us anything?

Red Hot in Black

As a black man who had grown accustomed to feeling somewhat like an outsider, whether home or away, I could be overly sensitive when it came to the skin I was in — not the quality of it (as they say, unfortunately, black don't crack), but the color of it.

Usually, though, I was certain that my righteous indignation was justified. Such was the case when my friend and roommate Rick made one of the most insulting racial comments I've ever heard that didn't start with an *N*. One of the reasons why I found what Rick said to be so alarming, and a large part of why I was so fond of him in the first place, was because I was certain that he was one of the least racist people I knew.

At the time, he loved R&B music more than any white guy I'd ever met, to the point where he often introduced me to semi-obscure black singers — N'Dea Davenport, Brand New Heavies (Davenport's on-off band), Mica Paris, Puff Johnson, Chantay Savage, Pauline Henry of The Chimes, among others — whom I otherwise might not have discovered until years later, if ever. He was the only white person I'd ever known — the only person *period* — who had a Miki Howard CD in his collection. If that didn't entitle him to a "ghetto pass," as John Mayer would say, nothing did.

He was equally color-blind when it came to dating. Black,

white, blue: If you were good-looking and smart, you had a shot with my friend Rick. Although he and I were never more than friends, I always sort of hoped I would find someone just like him in New York City, someone for whom my skin color wouldn't be the primary consideration if he approached me (or not) in a bar, in a club, on the street. . . . Someone who wouldn't talk to me about his fondness for black men . . . Someone who wouldn't show me pictures of ex-boyfriends who were all black . . . Someone whose eyes wouldn't linger too long on every halfway-decent black man we passed, occasionally exchanging loaded looks with ones I'd be certain he'd slept with . . .

One night Rick and I were having dinner at an Indian restaurant on 6th Street in New York City's East Village when we spotted something mouth-watering that wasn't on the menu. It was our waiter — tall and handsome, an Indian version of Enrique Iglesias — and we both wanted him for dessert. I figured Rick had the edge because in the United States, attractive white guys usually did, but when Enrique approached our table, he immediately focused his attention on me, asking questions and making flirtatious small talk. By the time I ordered the shrimp biryani, he was practically sitting on my lap.

At the time, I failed to mention that it wasn't the first time we'd met because, well, that was between Enrique and me. I'd gone to the same restaurant on the night of Christmas Day several weeks earlier, and he had been my waiter. It was my first holiday season in the big city, and since two of my three roommates, including Rick, and my few friends were out of town, I spent the day alone. At night, I schlepped from our three-level brownstone apartment in Jersey City, New Jersey, into Manhattan for dinner at the same restaurant on 6th Street's Indian row that Rick had introduced me to months earlier, shortly after my arrival in New York from Charlotte, North Carolina, where I'd spent the previous summer interning at the *Charlotte Observer*. So I guess you could say Enrique and I had history. I was considering explaining this to Rick when he suddenly morphed into the worst sport ever.

"I guess he likes darker guys," Rick sniffed as Hottie McWaiter walked away. I wasn't sure if Rick, feeling slighted because our server had barely acknowledged him, was taking a swipe at me, suggesting, like so many people abroad who assume that I'm hot stuff do (because I'm "exotic"), that no one could possibly be interested in me for reasons other than the color of my skin. Or was he simply speaking an unavoidable truth about black men and the nonblack men who found them attractive? Does a white man who wants a black guy *only* want a black guy? Are we all basically interchangeable?

I'll never know for sure what Enrique saw in me, but unavoidable truths about black and white became harder to avoid after I left New York City and moved to Buenos Aires. After years of being more or less invisible on the U.S. gay scene, where blue eyes and white skin ruled, for the first time in my life, I was the center of attention for reasons that had everything to do with my appearance. But it wasn't about my sartorial elegance, my winning smile or my piercing brown eyes so much as it was about the color of my skin. Well, maybe it was sometimes about the winning smile, but it was hard for me to tell when everywhere I went I heard the same things:

"Me encanta el color de tu piel!" ("I love the color of your skin!")

"Sos mi fantasia! Para siempre he tenido muchas ganas de estar con un chico negro!" ("You are my fantasy! I've always wanted to be with a black guy!")

"Es verdad lo que se dice sobre los chicos negros?" ("Is it true what they say about black men?")

In Australia and Southeast Asia, it was a lot more of the same, only usually in English. (During my frequent trips to Europe in the '90s, regardless of what people were actually thinking, my skin color rarely came up in conversation or got acknowledged in roundabout ways, which might have been one reason why it was my favorite continent.) In Bangkok, I once met a Malaysian man on holiday from Brazil who said to me, "You must have a big cock," in an attempt to win me over and into bed.

"And you must have a small one," I replied. One bad stereotype deserved another.

The Australian men who approached me in Melbourne

were as charming as they were attractive, and for the most part (usually offline), they were less crude than my sexual suitors were in Argentina and in Bangkok. But they, too, almost always managed to weave my skin color into their come-ons. Melburnian women rarely made overt racial references, but because so many of the females I encountered in Buenos Aires and Bangkok did, I always thought I knew what distaff Australians were *thinking* when they approached me. One Monday night at the Prince of Wales, a woman walked up to me and said, "Everyone in the bar is looking at you and wondering if you're gay or straight. So, which is it?"

Who? *Me?* I knew exactly why they were all looking, and why she'd come over to me. It wasn't because I was the red-hottest stud in the room or because of my gray, indeterminate sexual preference. Perhaps I was being too modest, or maybe I'd had too many people pull out the black card with me (and before our conversation was over, she would, too), but I was convinced that if I were white and the same level of attractive, I would have gone completely unnoticed. Although I was secretly pleased with the attention, it became less thrilling once I realized that it probably would have applied to any black man standing in my John Varvatos boots. It wasn't personal, and my wobbly self-confidence needed it to be.

One evening a year or so later, back in Thailand, I was exchanging texts with Jack, an American expat from North

Carolina living in Bangkok. When he asked about the time I'd spent in Australia, he made an observation that I'd heard way too often.

"Oh, man. I bet you get a lot of attention there," Jack wrote.

Here it comes again, I thought, trying to construct a clever comeback in my head. "I get a lot of attention everywhere." *There!*

"I'm not surprised. You've got a very handsome face."

What? No "black" comment? Now there was an unexpected twist! Although he had his own race thing — His boyfriend was Thai, and he was typically attracted to Asian guys only — he found me attractive for reasons that may or may not have involved my skin color. He never felt compelled to mention it, unlike another American I met in Bangkok.

"You know, I've never been with a black guy, and I never even really thought about it until I met you."

The New York tourist who was standing too close to me at DJ Station was talking as if he expected me to jump for joy right into his open arms. I pretended I hadn't heard him, but I'd heard it all before, in multiple languages, sometimes when the guys weren't even talking to me. *"Dos pijas negras!"* my friend Rob once overheard one Argentine marveling to another as they stared at the circus attraction — us, the two black guys — in Rheo, a Friday-night gay party in Buenos Aires. It was official: Rob and I had become our black penises.

We ignored them and resisted the urge to cause a scene. Just because they saw us as penises didn't mean we had to act like dicks.

Computer Love

Never had I felt more like a big black dick than on Grindr, the sex-first-ask-questions-later mobile app that prohibited me from showing mine even if I was willing to consider publicly exposing it.

Some of my friends, most of them in Australia, had been swearing by the efficacy of Grindr for months, whether you were looking for sex for breakfast, love in the afternoon, or a midnight snack. Occasionally, I'd been told, a boyfriend could be part of the deal. Dov, my American friend living in Melbourne, found two of his on Grindr. ("I went over there for sex," he told me shortly after hooking up with the first one, "and we just clicked.") Another mate, Craig, found true-blue love. Within weeks, he'd handed over a spare set of keys to his apartment and was spending the holidays with the family of his Grindr find.

Frankly, I remained skeptical about this mobile app where horny gay men were going in search of Mr. Right Now based on proximity. When I first heard about Grindr from my Melburnian friend Marcus a year and a half before I'd actually use it, I was pretty certain that it wasn't for me. Something about all those shirtless, faceless torsos anonymously angling for attention on an iPhone screen overwhelmed me. And a miniature keypad wasn't exactly conducive to real conversation. If I was going to meet up with a perfect stranger for drinks, dinner, sex or all three, it was imperative that we got beyond the "Hi. Top or bottom?" phase, which was far less likely when you and your would-be score were exchanging small talk on a keypad that was smaller than your palm. (Sometimes size *does* matter.)

But I was curious. Before I took the plunge on Grindr, I did my research. After reading the testimonials of friends who'd found love in that hopeless place, I interviewed two playwrights who'd written stage productions about Grindr, for an article I did for *Time Out Melbourne*. I wasn't particularly encouraged by anything either had to say.

"If you're looking for a boyfriend or a relationship, get the fuck off Grindr, mate. It's not going to happen," one of them told me. So the benefit would be? "It takes the awkwardness out of being rejected by someone face to face. If you meet someone on the dance floor and you buy them a drink and ask them if they're keen, and they say no, it really hurts. It's a slap on the face. But on Grindr, for some reason, there's this fake wall where nothing really hurts that much. If you say something to a guy and he's not into you, it doesn't really matter. It's like it doesn't count. It's not real."

Not exactly a ringing endorsement. But upon my return to Bangkok at the beginning of March 2012 after two summer months that felt more like autumn in Melbourne, I decided to try it anyway. A few things quickly became abundantly clear.

1. Thai guys on Grindr made Argentines and Aussies look like masters of sexual subtlety and paragons of restraint, which was no easy task. There's no circumstance under

which it's appropriate to begin a conversation with "big black dick" or "fuck me," but on Grindr in Bangkok, no opening line, it seemed, was too crude to use. I tried to tell myself it was the language barrier, and they were just incorporating an economy of words into their dialogue, but as a wise man once said (and if he didn't, he should have), when in doubt, lead with "hello." It never goes out of style.

2. Mr. Right (Now) probably wasn't hiding behind sunglasses, torso shots and pictures of beautiful sunsets — or beside fag hags. (As a general rule, I learned to be wary of third parties, including the ladies with whom boys twenty-five and younger sometimes posed in their profile photos, as if a wingwoman somehow made them seem straighter by association.) I had more than a few mystery men message me, and when they finally got around to showing their faces, rarely were their mugs suitable for framing. Why would I respond to a faceless suitor in the first place? To make sure I wasn't missing out on something good — at least, that was why I responded to the Brazilian posing with his back to me.

Him: *Hi.*

Me: *Face, please!*

Pleasant surprise: Although I wouldn't slip his photo into a picture frame, it didn't make me want to end the conversation, which wasn't really much of one.

Him: *Looking for?*

Me: *Cool guys to talk to, drink with and maybe sleep with, too.*

Him: *Cool... We too.*

Unfortunately, the friend in the photo with him, the one he sent after he'd secured my tentative interest, wasn't quite so picture-perfect. And although my years of threesomes and living dangerously were not entirely behind me yet, I was more willing to do windows than couples who I didn't meet entirely by accident on the dance floor.

On a somewhat related note, another guy, one I could have sworn I'd met in real life the last time I was in Bangkok, sent me the following message: *Hi, wanna fuck my friend?* The man in the photo was cute, but even as a newbie, I knew to avoid Grindr pimps and the tricks they were peddling.

3. Grindr brought out the stupid in many people who probably already had severely limited conversation skills; it was as if they spoke broken English, but it had nothing to do with language barriers. If they weren't treating hooking up like a cold, clinical business transaction between a prostitute and a john (see "Looking for?" above), only without the required exchange of cash, they were so unconcerned with formalities that they couldn't even be bothered to write complete sentences. I wasn't expecting Mark Twain's wit, but surely there were more exciting ways to keep a conversation flowing than "Cool."

4. Grindr made people disrespectful. Marcus told me about his friend Zoren, who used to respond to suitors he didn't like with a simple "Yuck." I didn't find Zoren particularly charming in person either, but apparently, his Grindr

etiquette really needed some work.

As I had been on Manhunt Australia, I was floored by how many Grindr profiles in Bangkok — almost always ones that originated Down Under — specified "Sorry, not into Asian guys generally." It would have been bad enough in Australia, but in Bangkok, shouldn't they have been showing more respect to the natives of the country that was hosting them?

5. Grindr was all about sex, which, if it was anything like those clumsy come-ons, wouldn't be worth getting out of bed — or into it — for. Love, or even normal conversation, would have to wait. A typical Grindr dialogue:

Him: *Hi. R u top or bottom?*

Me: *That's your opening line?*

Him: *Just curious. Sorry if it makes u inconvenient.*

Then, one evening about a week into my Grindr experiment, I had an epiphany. It was nothing life-changing, just an interesting observation/theory about the baser instincts of gay men. What if the number of crude opening lines I'd received over the course of seven whole days on Grindr had less to do with the application itself and more to do with what I wearing in my photo on it? Make that, *not* wearing.

In the digital snapshot, I was shirtless and wearing low-rise jeans, allowing for a bit of peekaboo underwear action. But because of Apple's standards of decency — no visible underwear, period — you could only see me from the waist up. So for all anyone knew, I might have been wearing nothing at all. How could they *not* look at me and only see a big black dick?

"Could it be," I asked Edward, the 24-year-old Russian expat I'd met on the app just a few hours earlier, "that because of my immodest pose, people were assuming that I was after only one thing, too?" In the previous twenty-four hours alone, the opening remarks thrown my way had run the gamut from "Hi" to "You got big black dick?" to "Do you want to fuck me?"! Maybe, like the rape victim in the eyes of some truly twisted people, I was getting exactly what I was asking for.

Edward considered, but not for long. "I don't think so," he offered. "All of those websites and applications are the same: Grindr, Manhunt, Gaydar . . ." He mentioned a few other ones I'd never heard of. "Guys go there looking for sex, so they'll say anything." In fact, he admitted, he found it kind of refreshing. At least you knew where they stood from the beginning. And anything was better than those boring "Hi" openers.

I understood where he was coming from, which didn't make the Grindr-speak seem any less crude. Though I had no idea what went on behind closed firewalls on most of the sites he mentioned, I was familiar with Manhunt and Gaydar. I'd been asked all of the expected questions on both: "Top or bottom?" "Looking for?" "Is it true what they say about black men?"

Yes, I'd read them all. But on Manhunt, I found that there

was generally a bit more content — at least coming from users who weren't on mobile devices and could easily type more than a few words at a time. Even "You got big black dick?" didn't seem quite so bad with two or three sentences surrounding it.

On Grindr, there was a shocking increase in shocking vulgarity. As I had been told by one of the playwrights in Melbourne, the one who'd written an entire stand-up act called *Grindr: A Love Story?*, there was something about that site. (More than a year later, I'd catch his live routine in which he talked about his scary encounter with a "big black bear" — in other words, his first time with a black man — one he *didn't* meet on Grindr.) Like all those other forums, most guys went there looking for one thing only, but despite the app's no-nudity clause that applied to profile photos, though not shared ones, something about the Grindr format (maybe the geolocation aspect?) was encouraging extreme behavior. This also might have held true for other similar meat-and-greet mobile-device apps, none of which I'd actually used.

Perhaps, I considered, this was just how things were in Bangkok, a city whose name was almost synonymous with sex (pronunciation: *bang-COCK!*), a place where locals would walk up to you in a bar and grab your crotch, thinking they were acting well within their gay rights. Maybe it had nothing to do with what I was wearing — excuse me, *wasn't* wearing — in my profile photo.

Part of me remained doubtful, though. I spent a couple of days pondering my hypothesis while fielding vulgar come-on after vulgar come-on. On the third day, I decided to try a new experiment. I switched the shirtless photo with a far more modest one in which I was seated at a dinner table, the only things naked being my head and my arms.

Immediately, I noticed a dramatic decrease in activity. During the first twelve hours or so, only about five guys messaged me at all, down from an average of five every fifteen minutes. Maybe the new photo wasn't that attractive. Perhaps it was just a slow Grindr day. Nobody called me "hot" or "sexy." Everyone opened with a simple "hello," except for one person.

Him: *Hey, man, where are you from?*
Me: *hey, i'm from the u.s. u?*
Him: *From indonesia. U work here?*
Me: *sort of. i'm a writer.*
Him: *What do u write?*

I couldn't believe what I wrote next.

Me: *google jeremy helligar and find out! :)*

That stupid smiley face and my arrogance surprised even me! But I was so tired of answering variations on "What do you do for a living?" online and offline. Plus, typing on an iPod Touch keypad was murder, so I wanted to keep my responses brief without resorting to typical Grindr-speak. But if I really put all kidding myself aside, I was probably partly trying to impress him and partly trying to get rid of him. Who would bother to check something like that, and who'd want to meet the person who tried to get him to do it?

Moments later, he responded.

Him: *Get out! You wrote for People mag and Entertainment Weekly???*

You would think he'd just witnessed the second parting of the Red Sea. He went on to name *EW*'s two movie critics, who had both been with the magazine seemingly since the first parting of the Red Sea. He couldn't believe I knew them.

Him: *I read Entertainment weekly religiously, man! I even have a copy right now from jakarta. This is huge!*

Now he was really saying something. I liked him already. A former devotee of *Premiere* magazine, he turned to *EW* after the former folded. Now he was addicted to it in Jakarta, where he said he worked in advertising (his "day job," as he put it, which had brought him to Bangkok) and wrote a movie column for a local magazine. I didn't know that *Entertainment Weekly* even existed in Indonesia!

Our exchange went on, until I couldn't bear to type another letter on that ridiculous keypad. Not once was there any talk of tops, bottoms, "fun" (Grindr lingo for sex) or dicks. By the end of the conversation, at which time we agreed to meet up at some point to share war stories before his Saturday departure, I was wondering if we would have had such an enjoyable chat, if he would have messaged me at all, if he would have cared what I did for a living, if I hadn't changed my photo. He later told me that he probably still would have messaged me, respectfully, of course.

So Why You Want to Give Me That Funny Vibe?

Late one Saturday night in Melbourne, my friend Dov made an interesting comment/observation that I filed away for future consideration when I wasn't slightly tipsy on vodka. I'm not sure how or why, but the conversation had suddenly shifted to being black and living in a place where you're a minority and a rarity, too.

It was a topic that had been broached several times by friends and acquaintances over the course of the previous year — in Melbourne, in Sydney, in Kuala Lumpur, in Bangkok — but I'd always tried to steer the conversation elsewhere, having had my fill of black talk in Buenos Aires, where I could never be sure whether someone was talking to me out of interest in me or out of curiosity about me, like maybe I would unbutton my trousers and let them see for themselves if it's true what they say about black men. Trust me, a few guys tried to find out for themselves.

Dov's comment, though, had nothing to do with size, or why I was going to a Soundgarden concert. Could I *be* less black? I had a feeling that's what he had been wondering earlier in the evening when I told him I'd gotten tickets. He seemed genuinely surprised, which, he explained, was because he just didn't think I'd be a fan, not because black people can't like Soundgarden. Having gotten over his shock over my love of '90s grunge, he'd moved on to the distinct aura he got from black men in bars and clubs when there were no other black people in the vicinity. The way he explained this funny vibe, it was an attitude like, "I can have anyone I want here, so why would I talk to *you*?"

I didn't know if anyone actually had ever said that to him, but at first, I wasn't sure what he was talking about. Maybe that was because I hadn't met enough black men in Melbourne, or in Bangkok, or in Buenos Aires, and those whom I had met hadn't exhibited any special behavior that I didn't notice when I was living in the United States. Black men in gay bars and clubs in pretty much every country, particularly ones from the U.S., always seemed to regard me either as a comrade or the competition, embracing me emphatically or shooting me suspicious looks, but they never pulled any of that I'm-too-cool-for-this-room-and-for-you stuff with me.

I wondered to what extent Dov's view of black barflies might have been clouded by his own preconceptions and personal bias. If they were white and fluttering around in the same manner, would he even have noticed? Or perhaps the attention they were getting might have influenced the way he saw them. Wouldn't any guy of any color surrounded by ardent suitors look a little bit like an asshole?

Then I started to worry. "Do *I* act like that?" I asked Dov. He assured me that I didn't, but I couldn't help but wonder how I came off to people who didn't know me, the ones standing off to the sidelines, too intimidated or too turned off to approach. Were they seeing me the way my friend saw black men who weren't me? And did I treat them like comrades or competition?

Several weeks earlier, I had received some interesting Aussie insight into my public persona while talking to the neighbor of my girlfriend Devarni. After complimenting my physical appearance several times, much to my discomfort and disarmament (it isn't every Sunday afternoon that a good-looking heterosexual male repeatedly comments on how attractive his new gay acquaintance is), he asked why I was single.

"Why do *you* think I'm single?" I was more interested in what he thought.

"Well, if I were watching you talk to me — smiling, animated, friendly — I'd think you seemed really cool and interesting. You'd definitely be someone that I'd want to talk to. But if I just saw you standing alone, I don't know. You're good-looking, you have a nice body, and with that cap on, you look like a really tough military guy. I might be a little bit afraid to approach you."

Military?!

Now there was a description I didn't hear too often . . . *ever* . . . at least not in connection to me. If I were white, I seriously doubt that my olive-green cap would have had the same effect. My new acquaintance must have read my mind because he immediately accused himself of objectifying me.

And although he stood by every single compliment he'd given me, he acknowledged that my being "exotic" in Australia might have a lot to do with how people perceived me.

In Bangkok, I saw the exotic anti-stigma in action every time I went to DJ Station. Average-looking men of European descent who probably got little to no attention back home were suddenly holding court with the cream of the Thai crop. Likewise, Asian men whose fellow countrymen might rarely have given them the time of day were suddenly being fawned over by white tourists and expats, the ones without a no-Asians dating policy. It was an interesting dynamic to watch, and I did usually sense a certain cockiness in the air, but what guy comes off as humble when he's being pursued from all sides?

One morning, I received an email from a photographer who had seen photos of me on my blog. "I have been on the hunt for the longest time to find a suitable black male model for my work. . . . Would you be keen?" he asked. If only it hadn't been for that five-letter word that starts with a *B,* my "Definitely, maybe" would have been a "Definitely, of course." But there was no escaping that *B*-word. Nearly six years after leaving New York City, I'd come to accept it as a simple fact of life and lust abroad. And anyway, a compliment was a compliment, no matter what color it was.

Who knew what people were seeing when they saw me? The less it mattered what they thought of me — a state of enlightenment that I was continuously striving to achieve — the less it mattered why. And if they were sizing me up from a distance, judging me with their eyes and not their ears, it was their loss. They didn't deserve what they wouldn't get.

I've Been Watching You Watching Me

No matter how often and how hard people stared, I was never going to get used to being a walking and talking attraction because of the color of my skin. For the four and a half years that I lived in Buenos Aires, almost on a daily basis, someone would stop me — in the bar, in the club, on the dance floor, on the street, on the *colectivo*, in the men's room (gross!) — and ask me to take a photo with them.

Once upon entering Sitges on a Friday night, it took me a full five minutes to get from the entrance to my friends on the inside because three different groups stopped and asked me to pose with them. Considering the minuscule number of black people in Argentina, I understood that bumping into one qualified as a truly Kodak moment. Rob got the same thing when he lived in BA; sometimes we got it together. That's just the way things were. Still, it took me a bit by surprise every time.

It's not like I blended into crowds any more in Australia than I did in BA, but for the most part, Aussies didn't seem to have the same need to document black-man sightings with a camera. (Although, a guy in Melbourne once took my photo as I ran past him while I was jogging around Albert Lake in St. Kilda.) The cameras didn't flash quite as blindingly in Thailand as they did in BA, but when they did, it was always a production.

Sometimes I wished for more anonymity, but I didn't

exactly object to attention when it wasn't accompanied by foolish questions about urban black myths. Although I'd never considered myself to be particularly photogenic, not once did I ever refuse a photo request. If I knew what was good for me, I probably would have gotten all diva up in there, though. "No photos, please," I would have insisted when entering every room. Who needed so many photos of oneself floating around the universe, unmanaged?

Despite my misgivings, I totally got why some people wanted to take a piece of me home with them. In certain parts of the world, where the color black is such a rarity among the general population (unless being worn as an article of clothing), bumping into a brother became an event of sorts. Bangkok's Grand Palace was there for every visitor to see, but not everyone got to run into a living, breathing black person while in town, or when in transit from one key tourist spot to another.

No wonder I didn't get a minute of peace on the ferry ride from Koh Chang to the Thai mainland during my first summer in Thailand. As soon as I sat down, a gaggle of middle-aged Asian women descended on me like I was the second coming of Will Smith. For the duration of the one-hour trip, they surrounded me, asking me where I was from and begging me to pose for photos with them. I had no idea what they were going to do with those snapshots. Would they take them home and slip them into slide shows to share with their friends the rare, exotic beast they'd encountered on the boat ride?

Would they frame them? Hang them on the wall? Use them as their new profile pics on Facebook? Was I being filmed, too? Would video of my new friends and me go viral on YouTube? One could only hope for the latter, at the very least.

I'd been recognized several times in New York City by people on the street who had seen me as one of those talking-head entertainment experts on networks like E!, Bravo and MTV. In Buenos Aires, Melbourne and Berlin, I had guys in nightclubs recognize me from the photos on my blog. (One of them, Rob in BA, became one of my best friends there.) I figured it was just a matter of time before some random stranger came up to me and said, "I think I saw you in one of my friend Mai Ling's photo albums on Facebook."

I could relate, to an extent, to the camera-wielding tourists who approached me because I'd been there. But I was more likely to reserve my memory-card space for photo ops with people like Kristin Scott Thomas and Robert Smith of the Cure after interviewing them or *Days of Our Lives* star Blake Berris after running into him on a crowded street in downtown BA. I never would have dared approach some random stranger, no matter how hot he was, for the specific purpose of taking a photo with him.

But at least the ferry ladies asked. Not so the fellow in Pattaya whose curiosity branched off into slight creepiness. He briefly entered my life when I went to the Thai Alangkarn Theater in South Pattaya for a panoramic-extravaganza-as-

Thai-history-lesson that was sort of like *The Lion King* with live elephants and fire. My date, a dancer in the drag show at the Copa, the hotel where I was staying in Boyz Town, had stood me up, and I was at the Alangkarn complex alone, one of a handful of Westerners surrounded by hundreds of Asian tourists.

After finishing the buffet dinner in the restaurant, I wandered out onto the patio for the pre-show entertainment, which featured singers, dancers and martial artists. I was starting to get into it when a large Indian man sat down next to me. Before I had a chance to move over, he was leaning in closer and putting his arm around me while his friend pulled out a camera. I knew exactly what to do. I smiled as his friend took the photo. Without saying anything, the man, who obviously didn't speak a word of English, or surely he would have asked for permission before invading my personal space (right?), grinned at me, nodded and gave me a thumbs-up before standing and walking away.

I wasn't sure whether to be flattered or appalled. Didn't he see the elephants by the entrance? They made for a far better photo op than I did. Unlike the elephants, though, I didn't charge twenty baht a snapshot. But maybe I should have. Of course, there'd always be a next time. And next time, if they expected me to smile, I decided, it just might cost them extra.

What You Gonna Do, Zimbabwe?

I wasn't going to say anything, but then I found myself talking to Ben, an African tourist who was a guest at Anantara Bangkok Sathorn, the five-star hotel I was calling home while I was living in that city. That's when it all came flooding out, everything about the odd question I had been asked the previous week.

As for the guy who got it out of me, Ben was thirty-two years old, and he'd spent the first eighteen years of his life in Zimbabwe before becoming a somewhat nomadic adult. Being a white person who had lived half of his years in a predominantly black society (his first language was Afrikaans, his second Swahili and his third English, which he didn't learn until he was sixteen), Ben approached race relations from an interesting angle. We dove right in.

He talked about some of the difficulties he'd had growing up in Zimbabwe, where his minority experience in some ways mirrored mine as a black kid in the United States. But what he said about the way Thai people reacted to his kind (a white African) was revelatory, leaving me questioning all of my positive impressions of them. Could there really be so much cynicism lurking behind those gleaming white smiles?

Ben told me about how his sister, who was living in Bangkok with her boyfriend, applied for a teaching job there before her arrival, and was asked during a preliminary telephone interview if she was a white African or a black

African. Apparently, black Africans needed not apply for teaching jobs within this particular organization, as a black African friend of Ben's had found out the hard, direct way during his own application process, which quickly tumbled downhill after he revealed that he was black.

Ben, who worked in marketing and owned his own company back home, also had faced this particular brand of discrimination against black Africans. He'd dealt with prospective business associates over the phone before his arrival who appeared to be visibly relieved when he showed up in person, presumably because he was white, an assumption Ben made based on precedent. According to him, "Are you a black African or a white African?" was a standard and perfectly acceptable question he'd heard numerous times when conducting business over the phone with potential Thai clients. Those who were afraid to ask might come up with some excuse not to do business with him and magically change their minds once they found out that he was white.

As I listened, I thought about all the people I'd met since I first came to Thailand. I'd never been in a country where people were more kind, and up to that point, I hadn't encountered any overt racism directed against me. But from the stories that expats told me about office rivalries between Thais and *farangs* (Thai slang for Westerners) and altercations with taxi drivers that turned violent, I sensed there might be another side to Thais, a darker side, one that I wasn't privy to because most of my daily interaction with them was on the level of customer to service provider. People were pretty much paid to be nice to me in Bangkok.

My dealings with the folks who didn't serve me had been mostly positive as well, but on a superficial level. They observed the traditional Thai code of conduct, but they didn't go out of their way to connect with me in any meaningful fashion, not the way some people had in Argentina and Australia, which I blamed somewhat on the language barrier. I hadn't even made a halfhearted attempt to learn Thai, and surprisingly, despite Thailand's high level of tourism and its international profile, people seemed to speak less English there than in any of the other Southeast Asian countries I'd visited, including Cambodia and Laos.

In the gay bars and discos, it was more of the same. When local guys talked to me, I sensed it was more out of curiosity about the exotic black guy — or, more accurately, my penis — than anything having to do with me as a person. Was it really as big as legend had it? I was basically a piece of dark meat, and white meat was clearly the preference. The bulk of them saved their attempts at deeper communication for the European white guys with blue eyes. That's what they really wanted.

Certain that he'd understand, perhaps even provide some valuable insight, I told Ben about the misgivings I'd been harboring for a week over a conversation I'd had with a Thai-Chinese guy who worked in the hotel. He and I had been on a hello/goodbye basis for months, always observing all the perfunctory niceties when we passed each other in the lobby or on the street or when we wound up in the same elevator, but one week earlier, when we were both enjoying a rare break in Bangkok's scorching heat and humidity poolside, we had an actual conversation for the first time.

"Jeremy, are you from Africa?" he asked halfway into it.

I was shocked. Not because it was an uncalled-for assumption, but because somehow, astonishingly, I'd never been asked that question before. During my six years living abroad, people had always assumed I was from anywhere but the motherland. In Argentina, I got (in the order of frequency) Brazil, Cuba, the U.K., France, occasionally even the United States. If only I had a peso for every time I was asked, *"Sos Brasilero?"* I'd never have to work again. In Australia, I generally got the United States, with some people actually pinpointing the Caribbean because as native English speakers, they recognized that my accent placed me outside the U.S. mainland.

In Thailand, though, the locals rarely made any assumptions about my origin out loud. It was usually "Where are you from?" without betraying that they had even the foggiest idea. So the hotel employee threw me off-guard when he asked if I was from Africa. Not just because I'd never gotten that question before, but also because I couldn't believe he had no idea. I thought everyone who worked at Anantara Bangkok Sathorn knew. It was sort of my thing around there, all anyone ever talked to me about. New York City this, New York City that.

"No, I'm from the United States. New York City, to be exact."

"Can't you tell by the way he talks?" his colleague Tong chimed in. "He has a classic perfect American accent."

Not really, but I didn't feel like arguing that point. I was still focused on the question. I wasn't 100 percent sure, but I thought I noticed a shift in the guy who'd asked it, one that would have been imperceptible to most naked eyes. There was something about the look in his, the way it changed from one moment to the next, after I revealed the truth about my origin.

"He was raising his opinion of you," Ben offered, taking the words right out of my mind. "He saw you as being more valuable because you are from the U.S. and not Africa."

I didn't want to think the worst of people — though I often did — but I had a hunch that Ben was probably right. It's why the conversation had been weighing down the recesses of my mind all week, and I felt that since Ben had finally said it, not me, there might be some justification for the way such a seemingly innocent but, in reality, terribly loaded question had made me feel.

One of my best acquaintances in Bangkok was a guy from Liberia and, shockingly, we'd never even broached the subject of race. I kept writing a memo to myself not to forget to have that uncomfortable conversation the next time I saw him. I stuck the mental Post-it to a spot where I wouldn't miss it. But I never did get around to it.

Coming from a place where he was part of the majority to one where he was among the minority, perhaps my Liberian friend was conditioned to have a completely different take on race relations in Bangkok than Ben's and mine. Every time I saw him at DJ Station, though, he seemed to be too concerned with the beat to care about the politics of black and white. Maybe those rose-colored sunglasses he always wore were good for more than dulling the glare of the strobe light. Maybe ignorance *was* bliss, especially when it came with a killer beat.

III. Eat Gay Love

About a Boy

Hey sexy man. This is Shane. I'm so glad I met you last night. Sorry I had to leave early with my friends. Let me know if you want to do something before you leave town. You're so hot LOL!

"Who the hell is Shane?" I asked myself after receiving a text message from him at 8:23 a.m. on a Friday morning at the tail end of my first trip to Melbourne one unforgettable October. Was he that twenty-one-year-old kid I'd met at The Peel about six hours earlier? But wait! Wasn't he there with a girl?

The beginning was not exactly what you'd call the start of a storybook romance. In fact, chapter one began with the girl who, I'd later find out, was Shane's increasingly insignificant other at the time. I was still stumbling through the mental fog of inebriation and couldn't recall the particulars of the circumstances under which we all had met. It may have had something to do with my pullover. When she zipped it down halfway and saw that I wasn't wearing anything underneath, she found it both scandalous and sexy.

Soon after, her friends had joined in on the fun. The rest was a blur. There was dancing. There was laughing. And by God, there was drinking — a lot of it.

Before their arrival, I had been dancing on my own (figuratively, not literally — yet), alone at The Peel Hotel. It was a big, gay dance club in Collingwood with no cover charge (typical north of the Yarra River, where minimum-waged hipsters and bohos in op-shop threads dominated), three bars, several chill-out sections, one of the best patio/smoking areas in Melbourne and a giant dance floor packed with extra-tall early twentysomething twinks dancing to the latest cheesy pop hits.

"Get sexy right now!"

DJ, hit that button, hit that button, spin me right round, baby, right round, like a record, baby, right round, round, round. In the absence of Dead or Alive's greatest hit pounding my eardrums, the youthquake of Sugababes' year-old single was exactly what I needed to hear to shake me out of my blue funk and lift my sagging spirits.

"'Cause I'm too sexy in this club
To sexy in this club
So sexy it hurts . . ."

My friends had gone home, and I was still smarting from a snubbing by Chris, a thirty-two-year-old blond businessman from England (and quite possibly the only guy in the dress-down barrio wearing a suit and tie after midnight) whom I'd met a few weeks earlier at the Prince of Wales Hotel, a pub way across the Yarra in St. Kilda.

Chris and I had kissed a little at Sircuit, a glorified cruise bar with multiple pool tables and instant-gratification rooms on the other side of a staircase that I never saw anyone ascend, a few blocks away from The Peel. It was still Thursday night at the time, and he'd made the sexy revelation that whenever he masturbated, he thought of our first makeout session at the Prince. But he still ended up leaving Sircuit with someone who wasn't me. I felt defeated, a loser in lust. I needed an ego boost badly.

That's when Shane's girlfriend came in. I was standing solo, in search of a temporary distraction in the standing area by the back bar, when she entered my scene bearing compliments.

"Are you really not wearing anything underneath?" She slowly pulled the front zipper of my pullover south. "Wow, you aren't! Hey, guys, come and look at this!" She was caressing my chest above the pullover on one side of the zipper with one hand and motioning for her entourage of four to join her with the other. I assumed they were a bunch of straight college students who had wandered into the gay club by mistake and stayed for the good music. Those Aussie boys were so rugged and masculine that my gaydar started to malfunction whenever I was around them, even, apparently, in gay clubs.

When she was finished propping me up, Shane, to whom she had introduced me by then, took over. While she and the other boys were on the dance floor, Shane and I sipped our drinks and shared stories. He was completely enthralled by the ones I told about my life and times as a journalist in New York City before moving to Buenos Aires four years earlier. Though I still figured he was straight, I must have given him my phone number, a detail I wouldn't have remembered if he hadn't sent me that text the next morning.

As I sat in the back of a taxi staring at the message, the mental fog began to lift just enough for memories of the previous evening — and of Shane — to start drifting into my spinning head in bits and pieces. Although we'd met in a gay bar, Shane had been the epitome of what people on gay dating websites called "straight-acting," and we'd maintained a respectable physical distance. Yes, there'd been some flirting on my part, but for me, that was a common side effect of too many whiskey and Cokes.

I couldn't recall the particulars of what we said (as I'd later find out, neither could he), but if what Shane eventually told me was true, he did most of the pursuing when his friends weren't looking. So why had I sized him up as straight, then? It didn't matter once he'd thoroughly outed himself with that text. I'd have to deal with him later, though. At the moment of his text's arrival, I was busy hitting on the taxi driver, a handsome young Sikh wearing a turban. He'd just finished telling me that he'd picked me up at The Peel (in his cab, not on the dance floor) and taken me home exactly one week earlier.

"You were with this guy," he said. "And he kept kissing you." I couldn't tell if he was disgusted or interested. "Do you remember?"

The guy? Yes. Him? Not one bit, though strangely enough, I remembered the taxi ride perfectly. How could I have forgotten a face like that? Had I been that drunk? I couldn't possibly have been more wasted than I had been the night before, under the influence of copious amounts of Jäger shots and whiskey. The night before, after Shane and his friends had gone home, I promptly forgot all about them, and ended up leaving The Peel with a pair of mates (as they say in Oz) — one tall, one short, both cute — and going to an apartment around a few corners, where the tall one lived. After an hour or two spent rolling around on a bed with both, the short one left to go to work and the tall one called me a taxi. What were the chances of my being a repeat customer of the driver?

As I leaned forward in the backseat and stroked his lap while listening to him recount our previous chance encounter, I thought about Shane's message on the phone that I was clutching like a bar of gold. Its unexpected arrival at just that moment must have been a sign — or so I thought at the time. The night before and the morning after were merging into one serendipitous adventure that told me I belonged to the city, *this* city: Melbourne, Victoria. That was when I decided that Buenos Aires and I were definitely through — for now. Melbourne was my brand-new lover. I'd been contemplating relocating from the moment of my arrival in Melbourne by eleven-hour train ride from Sydney more than a month earlier (It had me at "Welcome to Melbourne!"), but now my bags were as good as packed.

I'd find out months later, while Shane and I were drinking wine after eating the birthday dinner he'd cooked for me, that

I wasn't the only person whose so-called destiny was on the brink of being fulfilled that morning. Until the following evening when we had our first date, Shane had never been with a man. As I celebrated turning forty-two with my closeted boyfriend who was half my age, he told me that the young lady who'd played with my zipper and introduced him to me had been his girlfriend, though they were on the verge of breaking up at the time. The topper? When he'd texted me for the first time, he had been lying in bed next to her, his head spinning from all the booze, his crotch throbbing with desire, though not for the woman beside him.

"I don't think that guy Jeremy liked us very much," he recalled her saying a few days later. Well, he liked *me,* he'd thought in response, not daring to even hint at just how much.

I must have been somewhat taken by him to have handed over my phone number. (Though my booze goggles had led to some monstrous pickups along the way, excellent taste always seemed to prevail when I was giving out my number.) But my memory of Shane's physical attributes was pretty hazy during our first text session, when I entered my one-bedroom rental apartment on Clyde Street — a narrow side lane near St. Kilda Beach that was populated with bungalows and apartment buildings that, coincidentally, was only a few blocks from his own place — and invited him to come over that evening. Before putting him on my guest list, though, I asked for his last name so I could look him up on Facebook, just to be on the safe side. I was pretty confident he'd be cute, but I didn't want to ruin my final Friday night in Melbourne by spending it coming up with ways to avoid kissing a toad.

By the third or fourth photo, I was sold. "Jeremy, you did good," I said to myself before friending him.

When Shane showed up on time at 9 p.m. sharp, he was even better-looking in person than he was in his profile photo, which was pretty impressive, considering his delicate condition. He was tall and solidly built, with his demin shorts revealing thick, athletic legs and his dark-blond hair flopped over to one side and resting high enough on his forehead so as not to conceal his sad blue eyes. His head was still somewhere in the clouds, and his stomach too queasy to even consider sharing the pepperoni pizza that I ordered. It was his worst hangover ever, he'd tell me months later, and he couldn't believe he'd made it to my place — not just because I was a complete stranger (and a guy!), but because of how physically ill he felt while walking over.

I was glad he'd rallied and shown up for what wouldn't be just our first official "date" but a milestone occasion for us both. For me, he was the first guy I'd ever been with whom I met when he was with his girlfriend. The fact that at twenty-one, Shane was twenty years my junior became less significant in my mind, sitting beside that major revelation. He may have been my youngest boyfriend ever, but he was born only seven months and six days after Gejo, the twenty-one-year-old Argentine I dated for several intense weeks shortly after turning forty, whom I dumped on the opening weekend of *Transformers: Revenge of the Fallen*, when he chose the Saturday midnight showing over me.

For Shane, that night was a game-changer for the simple reason that I was a guy. As he also revealed on my birthday (after the part about his ex-girlfriend's role as unintentional matchmaker), when we hit the sheets and the shower and the bathtub for the first time, it had been his first real sexual experience with a man, which, come to think of it, very well may have been another first for me. It wasn't normally just my luck to have to break in virgins.

I almost didn't do it that time either. On the night of our first date, when I asked Shane what had drawn him to me at The Peel and he responded, "You're hot, you're tall and you're black," the final part of his answer made me cringe, and I almost rang the bell, game over. But I decided to keep playing along. At least he hadn't asked if it was true what they say about black men, and he'd never again acknowledge the color of my skin unless I did first.

There was one particular image from the first few days after we met that embedded itself into my memory. Shane was leaving my apartment, and in one hand he was holding an oatmeal-raisin cookie I had given him, and in the other he was holding his school supplies. That was the moment when I knew I could fall in love with him.

Some people have a thing for bad boys, and I was always one of them, but my strongest weakness might have been the man-child, the proverbial paper tiger. I wanted to take care of Shane. Meanwhile, I wanted him to wrap his big strong arms around me and protect me. He was so young and dewy, almost like the most adorable puppy. Every time I saw a cute baby or a cute animal or a cute cartoon, I thought about Shane. At the same time, he was big and solid and masculine, a guy who could lift me off the ground and carry me to the bed, which he did — twice!

Four days and three overnight dates after the first one, I went to Sydney for two days before returning to Buenos Aires. I had no idea where this thing with Shane would lead, and if I hadn't resolved to return to Melbourne even before he and I had met, I probably would have let it go. Months later, through many twists and turns, ups and downs and his shocking first "I love you" in early May, my future with Shane still remained uncertain. But in that taxi ride, as I was coming on to the cab driver and reading Shane's text message, who would have guessed that he would have such staying power? He was so young, so inexperienced, so in the closet. And we had met through his girlfriend!

When Shane and I clicked again upon my return to Melbourne at the beginning of March and tentatively became a "we," I knew it would be a total disaster or the start of something huge. Either way, I was certain it was going to be one of the stories of my life.

The Things We Do for Love

There's no tall, dark stranger quite so alluring as one who fancies himself an artist. Be prepared to work for him, though — and not just because of his brooding all-black demeanor and hot-and-cold temperament. All significant others come with special requirements, but get involved with someone who sings, plays music, acts or creates for a living, and you have to be nearly as committed to what they do as they are. The same goes for writers, that society of neurotic misfits and overthinkers to which I belong.

Shane, a self-described nonreader, could never be bothered to read anything I wrote, neither my blog posts nor my freelance articles on everything from pop culture to travel to, occasionally, sex and the city I happened to be calling home at the moment. Or so I thought, which was understandable, since he never commented on them or "liked" them on Facebook. Then during one email confrontation in which I accused him of not caring enough about me to care enough about what I do to read it, he dropped a bombshell: "I've read heaps of your s**t."

Oh.

I wasn't thrilled that he had referred to the writing that consumed so many of my waking hours as "shit," but Shane never did have a way with words, which might be why he found reading them so tedious. I was shocked on too many levels — He thinks it's "shit"? He *reads*? — to ask if he got my thinly veiled references to him, or if he was bothered by my thinly veiled dalliances with other people, which, technically, wasn't cheating because Shane and I had never gotten around to defining what we were exactly or to declaring exclusivity.

Although he'd come out to his older brother and a girlfriend (one of many platonic ones, which should have been a dead giveaway to anyone who was paying attention), he was still cowering so far back in the closet that being seen in public with me made him visibly uncomfortable. He told me that in Gippsland, the rural part of southeastern Australia where he grew up, men were ruled by a macho mentality. Being gay simply wasn't an option. I knew I was the starter boyfriend, the one who rarely got to reap the post-coming-out benefits, and until he put a ring on it, or at least had the courage to kiss me in public, I wasn't going to put all of my chocolate-covered eggs in his basket.

So I probably didn't have any right to expect him to read my "shit," and perhaps it would have been best if he hadn't. That way, he wouldn't have had a clue about what I occasionally got up to when he wasn't around, the guys I sometimes encountered online or around the very same spot where he and I had met, by the back bar at The Peel. They were the tall Aussie strangers who provided fodder for the odd provocative blog post (e.g., the Australian who hated Asians who tried to pick up the black guy). If he actually read those stories, none of which ever explicitly mentioned any untoward behavior (for despite the revelations in this book, I do know how to exercise discretion), if he was bothered by my nocturnal escapades on the nights when he was out doing his own thing, too, he never let on.

Only months earlier, during another argument, this one by text, he'd pretty much dismissed my life's work completely. "Maybe I'd be interested if you wrote something about me," he blurted out (via SMS). That might have been the first moment when I *knew* we wouldn't last. If strangers and people who barely knew me were more interested in what I did and what I thought than someone who claimed to love me, what were our chances of making it to December?

As much as I hated his insouciance, I knew it was easier for me to assume the role of the perfect boyfriend who was thoroughly invested in him and *his* work. Shane was a design student, and even if I hadn't been interested in his university projects, it wouldn't have taken much effort for me to flip through the pages of his portfolio and pretend to care. He'd probably never expect me to wear items from his latest line, and if I ever had to go to one of his fashion shows, at least there'd be booze and hot models to keep me entertained. (Thank God his specialty was menswear!)

But what if I had been dating a rocker and hated his music? Try breaking *that* to a moody artist! And even if I loved my rocker boyfriend's work, I still couldn't imagine having to live through his creative process, sit through all those gigs, applaud after every song, and pretend that I was happy to be supporting him in the crowd when I'd much rather be propped up on a barstool anywhere but there.

    Dating was always more complicated for me because of my attraction to Creative Guy. He was right up there with Bad Boy and Man-Child on the list of things I couldn't resist. We shared common ground as art lovers, and we had conversation potential, but being with Creative Guy came with career responsibilities that had everything to do with *his* job. It would be so easy to date a banker because he'd never bring his work home, and even if he did, I wouldn't mind an evening spent looking at cash. But as pleasing to the eye as the color of money might be, what in the world would we talk about while we were staring at it?

    My first boyfriend, Derek, was a painter, a then-unsuccessful one. Going out with him was relatively painless because experiencing his work required a minimal time commitment. I could look at every new canvas for a minute or two and improvise some insightful point of view. Derek was into painting donkeys at the time, so coming up with scintillating analyses to apply to representations of a basically unremarkable beast could be challenging, but at least I didn't have to get dressed and go anywhere. Eventually, I even grew to like asses.

    Accompanying him to museums and vintage churches in New York City, Boston, Barcelona, Madrid and the south of France was possible only with some physical exertion, but I was in love, so I tagged along cheerfully. I genuinely enjoyed the Museo del Prado in Madrid, and I even read biographies of Willem de Kooning, Vincent Van Gogh and Paul Cadmus. I never got around to those books on Pablo Picasso and the two Franciscos — de Goya and de Zurburán. Thankfully, we broke up before I had to.

Hooking up with a fellow writer would have been trickier because it's harder to wing it when reading and concentration are involved. That might be why I never seriously considered dating one and why I sort of felt for anyone who seriously dated me, even Shane. But then journalists and bloggers are like the singles acts of writing, cranking out the written equivalent of four-minute pop songs. "5-Star Bathroom Sex: Grindr and the Meat-Market Workplace" may have lacked the infectious hooks of Katy Perry's latest hit, but readers could be in and out of a one thousand-word article or blog post and "like" it on Facebook in fifteen minutes tops.

Falling for a novelist would have demanded much more effort, and not just because of my preference for nonfiction. I would have had to move each latest book to the top of my to-read list just because he was the love of my life. Then I'd have to read it, too! I'd rather wait for the movie, which would have made dating an actor easier, except the ones I met always performed on stages, not in films or on TV, which meant I couldn't download their work and watch it while multitasking at home. I'd gone to see so many dreadful Off-Off-Broadway productions starring friends and acquaintances that I would have done anything to avoid having to ever sit through another one.

Should true blue love have made all these points moot? When you really love someone, should you automatically be interested in what they do? I'd never gotten serious with a musician or an actor, but if I had fallen deeply in love with one, would I automatically have wanted to catch every show or see every play? I always had something of an aversion to poetry, so would falling for someone who wrote it for a living have reversed my fear of rhyming prose?

Maybe the support of platonic friends, family members and strangers who approach creative guys in clubs should be enough. I was out one night at The Peel with my friend Dov about three months after moving to Melbourne, when I noticed someone staring at me across the bar. Moments later, he was standing beside me, still staring.

"Do you have a blog called Theme for Great Cities?"

"Yes, I do. How do you know it?" I was playing it cool while practically hyperventilating on the inside.

"I came across it recently when I was looking for travel information about Buenos Aires. I love reading your stories, mate."

The handsome fan boosting my ego and my spirits had recognized my face from one of the photos on my blog. Dov wanted to see what the fuss was about, so he asked for the URL to check it out. I didn't think he actually would, but when I talked to him a few days later, he had so thoroughly read through it that he brought up things I didn't even remember writing. Either he had a surplus of free time, or he was genuinely interested in my life's work. That would have made at least two people in Melbourne. Too bad neither of them was my boyfriend.

Mad Love

Lord knows I have my shortcomings, but a lack of self-awareness has never been one of them. I am fully cognizant of the fact that at times, I can be endlessly annoying, and patience is not a virtue with which I've been blessed. My mother once told me that I give up on people too easily. My brother Alexi once said that my standards and expectations of people are too high. And I'm always telling myself that I don't know when to shut up.

Those who know me well might agree with my mother and brother (I do), and anyone who's ever disagreed with me probably would concur that sometimes I'd be better off zipping it. But I'm too typical a Taurus: headstrong and opinionated. I think first, talk later, and then I talk some more.

My friends love and loathe me for all of those strong qualities (or perhaps it's my loyalty, another quintessentially Taurean trait), but most importantly, they accept me as is because, you know, that's what friends do. Friendship with me is not for those who don't like to be contradicted or those who prefer their conversations to remain below volume five. A boyfriend once asked me why I have so much invested in being right all of the time. "Well, if I don't think I'm right, who will?" I responded. Why open your mouth if you think what you're saying is possibly wrong? Don't shoot the messenger because he speaks with great conviction above a polite whisper.

But talking about the passion (mine), if I have a point of view (which, in the strictest sense of the term, can be neither right nor wrong anyway, just informed or misguided), I feel compelled to share it. That goes double when the wheel of fortunate conversation topics stops on a subject I really care about. Racism and homophobia are guaranteed to rile me up, but nothing gets me going like music, movies and pop culture.

I once had lunch in New York City with Sharleen Spiteri from the Scottish band Texas, and as we looked at the restaurant's view of the Rockefeller Center ice-skating rink, she told me that the night she met her then-boyfriend and the future father of her daughter, they were arguing about rock 'n' roll. It was love at first fight!

So when does a conversation or discussion go from being heated and turn into a full-blown argument, the kind that can kill a relationship, not kick it off? Probably when tempers flare, but even then, not all arguments are created equal. An argument enters a danger zone only when it gets personal. That's when we strike nerves by hurling insults and saying things we can't take back but later wish we could. Sometimes a slap is thrown in, or a drink gets tossed in someone's face. But that's more likely to happen on *General Hospital*.

One night, Shane and I had a heated discussion about TV presenters in Australia. My feeling was (and is) that they are pretty awful, and his reflected his usual blind devotion to all things Australian: "Don't slam my country!"

"Don't take it personally," I pleaded. It was just that I could understand why the Australian media had to work so hard to brand *Today* cohost Karl Stefanovic, who really is no Matt Lauer, a superstar. No other country would!

In all of my months in Australia, I had yet to see a single news presenter with even a fraction of Diane Sawyer's teleprompter-reading panache. No wonder none of Australia's TV personalities had international profiles. (Sorry, Kylie Sandilands, you're no Howard Stern!) No wonder everyone there made such a fuss over Oprah Winfrey's 2010 trip to Oz. No wonder you could watch Ellen DeGeneres, Dr. Oz, Dr. Phil, David Letterman, Craig Ferguson and the ladies of *The View* every day on TV there. Australians had their own icons, but unlike the Oprah Winfreys and Simon Cowells and Graham Nortons of the world, their beloved television personalities didn't translate outside of the Aussie pop-culture vernacular.

I didn't direct any personal insults at Shane, smack him or throw my glass of water in his face. I was simply confounded. How did these marginally talented people get their TV jobs when I, an accomplished magazine editor from New York City, couldn't even get one rinky-dink Aussie publication to sponsor me? Shane struggled to come up with a valid counterpoint to my criticism of the Australian media but couldn't.

"I don't care about this," he sniffed, waving me away like a pesky gnat in the middle of my next point. "I don't want to argue about it anymore."

"Who's *arguing*?" I asked. "We're having a conversation. At least, I'm trying to!"

I figured he was just tired from an overload of schoolwork, so I tried to let it go. But how dare he just dismiss me like that? I understood that some people don't do debates. They'd much rather watch a boxing match or a good old catfight between two spunky divas on TV than get their hands dirty disagreeing with someone in real life. I got that raised voices turn some people off. But we all disagree sometimes, and sometimes when we do, we talk above a whisper. Hold it in now, and there's always the danger that it will come out later in an inappropriate setting.

Passion has its place outside of the bedroom. And regardless of where you stand on the subject of whether it's polite to raise one's voice in the presence of company, one thing's for certain: It's worse to interrupt someone midsentence, especially to announce that the conversation is over.

Unfortunately, I never got around to sharing any of these thoughts racing through my mind because Shane shut down, which, of course, made me angrier and resulted in what even I couldn't deny was a full-blown argument. The irony? There were no insults traded, no raised voices. In fact, barely a word was spoken. But nearly eight months after we'd met, we were having our worst argument yet. I was infuriated by his dead silence when there was so much more I wanted to say — about the subject that had started it, about him and his lousy attitude, about '70s TV stars whose hair never moved. I hated screaming matches, but surely shouting would have been preferable to the blaring silence!

By then, the cold fronts were moving in on our relationship with increasing regularity. Shane was so young, so I let things go, like his extreme inconsistency, that I wouldn't have overlooked with past loves. One week he acted like he couldn't get enough of me; the next, he was indifferent and mostly silent. I could set my watch or my calendar by his pattern of behavior. Had I played the needy boyfriend, he probably would have been right by my side. But that's not my style. Instead I'd send him nice text messages to let him know that I was thinking about him and wait impatiently for him to thaw.

We had a few text-message arguments over his lack of attentiveness during those times when his mood was below freezing. "I don't have time for this," he'd usually write, or something equally brutal and cold. He could be a cunt (his word), and he'd be the first to admit it and apologize for it when he was back to loving me again. I wasn't a doormat. I fought back. But I always stopped short of pulling out the heavy artillery that had blown away so many ex-boyfriends.

I always knew that I was putting up with more than I should have, or would have under different circumstances. Had

Shane and I met in New York City, or even in Buenos Aires, chances were I would have shown him the way out after the first cold front, but he was the closest thing I had to a home in Melbourne. I was having a difficult time adjusting to life among the Aussies, so cheerful and chatty yet so emotionally distant. We weren't quite connecting.

Someone once explained to me that the typical Aussie attitude was that if they weren't sure you were sticking around, why bother? Maybe Shane was struggling with that — getting closer, then pulling away in order to avoid being hurt by what he saw as my inevitable departure. In the end, it both hastened my exit and prolonged my absence.

I spent such an inordinate amount of time trying to decipher his mixed signals, determined not to give up on him, partly because I felt I had no other choice. He was my only real connection to Melbourne, a city I still loved although it was as hot and cold with me as Shane was (and not just because there can be four seasons in a day there). If I had let him go, I wouldn't have had any solid reason to stick around, since the job search wasn't panning out. In four months, I didn't get a single offer. If I had broken up with Shane, I probably would have called off the search as well, which would have meant admitting failure.

All that said, what I felt for Shane was real — at least, it felt real. The best part of our relationship, possibly the reason I fell so hard for him, was that we were so good together on a physical level — not sexually speaking, but in the sense of when we were inhabiting each other's personal space. Sure, most of our romance played out with us living on different continents, or behind the closed doors of whatever Melbourne rental I was calling home at the time. Sure, he never invited me over to his place because his roommates couldn't know about me. (Once, when he wanted to come over after a night of partying with them, he had to sneak out so that they wouldn't ask questions.) And sure, I'd met only one of his friends. But when Shane and I were together, it was magic.

He always gave me his undivided attention, rarely even looking at his phone, and never answering it when it rang, except for one time when his dad called while we were walking down Chapel Street to KFC. He had neither the gift of gab nor a gift for pinpointing my erogenous zones, and he could be moody and sullen. But when we were spooning in bed together, or cuddling on the couch watching his *The Secret Diary of a Call Girl* DVDs, and he was being gentle, attentive and loving, stroking my head or simply holding my hand, I had no reason to nitpick. I had everything I needed.

Or so I made myself think. I wanted more than after-work get-togethers and late-night booty calls, and had I been completely honest with myself, I would have realized that I wasn't blameless. Had I taken the initiative and insisted that we do daytime things and go outside our norm, he probably would have gone along with me. But part of me didn't want to because I was afraid I would realize how little Shane and

I actually had in common. We only seemed to truly connect when there was a physical, romantic component. The idea of going to a museum with him, or hanging out in a mall with him, or even sitting across the table from him in a restaurant (something we did only a handful of times and only once not in a fast-food joint), made me nervous.

Those were things I used to do with all of my previous boyfriends, but I couldn't imagine having that kind of relationship with Shane because whenever he was with me, he was like the walking dead. I had trouble communicating with him on a nonromantic level because he didn't communicate. He was a reactor, the kind of person who commented on things and recounted events, but he didn't dig deep. I don't believe he ever started a single conversation we ever had. Part of it may have been his age, but most of it was his character. While it contributed to his allure — the distant, brooding, sexy lover — it kept us from becoming real friends.

I did have to take some of the blame, though. He was who he was, but I never pushed him to connect with me on another level, thus inadvertently setting our status quo. I'd created my own monster. But if our first face-to-face clash, over something as inconsequential as Australian TV presenters, was any indication, maybe we were better off keeping it light. At least then I wouldn't have to sit up in bed looking at the back of his head while he pretended to be trying to sleep.

After reciprocating his silent treatment for a half hour, I tried to make nice: "Are you hungry? Do you want something to drink? Can I get you anything?" I was bending over backwards and sideways because I was going to Auckland the next day for the weekend, and I didn't want to spend our last night together fighting. All I got from him were monosyllabic grunts. I put up with it for another half hour, and then, for the first time ever, I completely lost it with him. Being young was no excuse for being such an ass. Without raising my voice, I told him I thought he should go. He did.

It wasn't the end of the world, or the relationship. The next morning, when I was on my way to the airport, he sent me a text message wishing me a good trip. He called me later that evening, drunk, of course. When we weren't physically together, a wasted Shane was always a nicer, more attentive Shane. The first time he told me he loved me — actually, he texted it in the middle of the night — booze gave him the courage. When we were apart and he was bombed, I didn't doubt how much I meant to him. But he couldn't spend all our time apart drunk off his ass.

I was still pretty upset over our fight when he called, but I didn't give him a hard time. I let him act like nothing had happened. In his mind, nothing had. He later told me that he had the same dynamic with his friends. He got upset, stewed for a few hours, then he was over it. I wondered if he was so hot and cold with them, too, and if he was always apologizing to them for being an "insensitive dick," which, once again, were his words, not mine. I couldn't imagine anyone but me being stupid enough to put up with it. But I was in love, and it was making me do dumb out-of-character things.

When we kissed and made up in person a few days later, I finally got to finish the thought that he'd so rudely interrupted. It was something about how my being a media person meant that analyzing and discussing TV personalities was right up the alley of things that interest me. He listened politely and apologized for being a jerk. I accepted his apology and promised myself that the next time I felt the spark of passion igniting inside of me, I'd try to keep it down. That was one vow I knew wouldn't go unbroken for long.

Rising Desire

On the day I met Malcolm, I was once again cross with Shane. He'd showered me with love and affection in the days leading up to my departure from Melbourne two months earlier, but since I'd arrived in Asia for what I had intended to be a one-month holiday in Thailand and other key destinations (Singapore, Malaysia and Vietnam), I could feel him slipping away, or maybe moving on.

That, come to think of it, was exactly what he threateningly said he would be doing in an email he sent to me at the beginning of October 2011, shortly after I'd set my third new Bangkok-to-Melbourne departure date: January 3, 2012, almost exactly six months after my July 5 arrival in Bangkok.

It was the first time he acknowledged the void I'd left in his life and expressed any hint of fear that I might not return to him. I convinced him to be patient with me without letting myself appear too vulnerable. I was as angry at myself as I was with him, because he wasn't the only one who was always holding back. But how could I lay down my heart at the feet of a man who wasn't even comfortable being seen with me in public?

I wanted to go back to him, but not the way we were. I wasn't sure what I was hoping to accomplish by staying away. Maybe I figured I could never have him completely, at least not while he still was struggling to figure out who he wanted to be, and on which side of the closet door. It would be easier to let the relationship expire from the relative emotional safety of another continent.

Had he given me one good reason to return to Melbourne, though, I never would have extended what was supposed to be a four-week holiday in Southeast Asia by one month, then by two, then by five — including a temporary three-month residency in Bangkok, a place I'd never even dreamed of visiting until it made such an auspicious appearance in *The Hangover Part II* the previous May. I was also sticking around partly because it was so cheap to live in Southeast Asia (with the glaring exception of spotless, soulless, overpriced Singapore) that it made financial sense. Being in Melbourne without a job had been rapidly depleting my savings. But had Shane snapped out of his apparent torpor of indifference, acted like he couldn't go another week without me, I would have dropped everything and gone running back to him. We could work out all of those other issues later, and I'd just try harder to find a job.

By the time I went to Manila at the end of August, Shane and I were talking only sporadically, usually when I sent him a text message or when he initiated a Facebook chat by saying "Hi" and not much else. After he blew off an amorous Friday-night text message from me, I was done trying to be good. I hadn't been exactly living the life of a saint over the course of two months in Southeast Asia, but I was no longer going to feel guilty about hooking up with a good-looking guy. We'd never discussed monogamy anyway, and even when I was in Melbourne, I wasn't naive enough to think that all of those drunken nights he spent out with his friends ended with him alone in bed, dreaming of me.

Enter Malcolm, who found me on Manhunt shortly after I arrived in Manila on a Thursday evening. He was cute, and he seemed nice enough. He would have been the perfect antidote to my rising ire over aloof Shane, but I spent the weekend blowing him off. When he messaged me on my last day in town asking to meet up, I finally relented. Unfortunately for him, our timing — 2:30 p.m. on a Tuesday — was all wrong. The last thing I wanted that day (or any day, to be perfectly honest) was love in the afternoon. I was all about sex for breakfast.

What I *was* looking for was to kill a few hours in Manila between my 2 p.m. late checkout from Antel Spa Suites and my 11:15 flight back to Bangkok. We arranged to meet at 2:30 at the Starbucks in Ortigas Center. What was the worst thing that could happen? He might be a total jerk, but I'd still get to see another part of the city. I arrived at the appointed meeting spot on time, and he was waiting for me outside of Starbucks. We shook hands, and he asked if we could go to his car and talk. Why there? He said his cousin was inside Starbucks, and he was trying not to be seen.

Oh, just what I needed: another closet case. But that's not the only reason I was reluctant at first. I kept hearing voices in my head. They belonged to my friends, and they were repeating those horror stories about Americans being kidnapped in the Philippines and held for ransom. I looked at Malcolm. What could this baby-faced guy wearing braces possibly do to me? I sat down but kept the car door slightly ajar.

We engaged in the perfunctory getting-to-know-you small talk. He told me all about Ortigas and the nearby attractions I'd missed by spending the previous four days exclusively in Makati and Malate. He asked me about my writing and told me he'd like to read my blog sometime. I wrote down the name and the URL on a piece of paper and handed it to him. He took it from me and reached into his bag and pulled out three stacks of yellow and green pens. The yellow ones read *Prozac* and the green ones read *Cialis*. (Foreshadowing!)

"These are for you," he said. "You're a journalist, so maybe you will need them."

Random, but cute. I shut the car door. After a bit more chitchat and a moment of uncomfortable silence, he got down to business. "You know, there are a lot of hotels and motels around here." He looked at me like I was going to be his late lunch. I knew exactly what he was getting at.

"Well, I just checked out of a hotel, so the last thing I want to do right now is go back to one," I said with a chuckle. "And it's so nice out today." Indeed, it was the first day since my arrival in Manila that the sun had bothered to come out. I wanted to enjoy it while it lasted.

He seemed to catch my drift, but then again . . .

"Ah, OK." Pause. "So . . . do you want to have some fun?"

I struggled to hold in my laughter. I asked him why everyone who was on the prowl in Manila talked like that, not yet realizing that "fun" was the new international gay euphemism for sex. Why was one even needed? I supposed that "fun" sounded more, well, *fun* than "Wanna fuck?" Still, I would have preferred an expression that didn't make me think of slides and monkey bars, especially from guys who looked like they were only a few years removed from them.

"Do you want to have some fun?" he asked again, apparently hoping for a different outcome.

This time I leveled with him. "Actually, no. I only have a few hours left in Manila, and I want to do a little bit of shopping and get something to eat afterwards." I felt kind of like a tease, but it's not like I'd promised him a rose garden, or a roll in one. I was hoping he wouldn't want to tag along.

He was disappointed, but he was such a good sport that I almost considered backtracking. He asked what I'd like to do then. He offered to take me to Robinsons Galleria, one of the nearby supermalls, but he couldn't go inside with me because he had a lot of friends who worked there, and they'd ask questions.

"What questions?" I played dumb.

"Like who you are. They know all of my friends, so if they see me with a guy they don't know . . ."

Yeah, they'd put one and one — him and me — together and arrive at the truth. This road we were headed down was an all-too-familiar one. I understood, and I was beginning to understand Shane a little better, too. Malcolm started to back out of the parking space.

"I'm really sorry," he said. "The reason I'm being like this is because I took some Cialis, and I'm really horny and really hard."

"What?" I asked. I'd heard him clearly, but I hadn't been expecting him to say *that*. I thought it was kind of presumptuous of him to think that I would be a guaranteed score. And furthermore, wasn't he a bit young to be popping Cialis? At least the pens finally made sense.

"Do you have erectile dysfunction? At your age?" I couldn't believe the words that were coming out of my mouth.

"No," he said with a laugh, and explained that he'd gotten the pills — and, presumably, the pens — from a friend who was a pharmaceutical rep. I thought that a nursing student in year one of a master's program should have known better, but I held my tongue. I glanced in the vicinity of his crotch to see if there was any evidence — exhibit E, for erection. Nothing.

"Are there side effects?" I felt like we were filming an infomercial.

"Yeah, there are some. Like, you get a headache. But I'm fine."

I'd always wanted to try it myself, and I already had a slight headache. For a split second, I thought, This is my chance. But I wasn't in the mood for "fun." I knew the libido enhancer would make me want it as much as Malcolm did, and I kept thinking of the episode of *True Blood* in which Jason Stackhouse overdosed on V Juice and ended up critically rock-hard in the ER. With my luck, that would be me!

"Well, if you decide later on that you'd like to meet up before your flight, give me a call," Malcolm said, interrupting my inner monologue.

"Sure."

"Do you think you'll come back to Manila?"

"Definitely."

"Cool. Next time you are in Manila, we'll have to go out one night for drinks."

And fun?

He didn't have to say it. I understood him perfectly.

What's My Age Again?

Alan wasn't buying what I was selling, which, in this case, was my real age. But then, no one ever seemed to. I didn't know whether it was because black don't crack (a cliché I'd come to loathe), the power of Kiehl's, genetics or a lucky combination of all of the above.

"I don't believe you are forty-two? You don't look it at all."

"But if I were going to lie about my age, which I've never done, why would I pick forty-two? I'd go down, not up."

"I guess that's true."

I could tell he still wasn't buying it, but by then, he was out with the "old" and on to new business: my body and my singing voice. He was impressed with both, which told me that he must definitely be either hearing-impaired or this was his idea of foreplay. Who cared? It was working. I took the compliments and ran — though not too far.

One-half Chinese and one-half Thai, Alan was the 25-year-old doorman at Copa showbar in Pattaya, Thailand. If he hadn't won me over with his sex appeal, he did when he asked to see my ID to confirm that I was a day over twenty-eight. No, he didn't quite have me at hello, but somewhere between refusing to believe my age and squeezing my bicep, he got me. Considering how beautiful he was, I wasn't sure how it possibly could have taken me three days staying at the adjacent hotel before I had even noticed him.

But once I had, I wasn't letting him out of my sight. "We'll be together tonight," I told my new Australian friends the next night, echoing Sting in one of his solo hits from the '80s. What followed was an evening of flirting and kissing in front of Copa showbar's entrance while Alan was on the clock, and melon margaritas at Nab, my favorite club in Pattaya, once he was off. During the tuk-tuk ride home, he wasn't afraid to hold my hand, although we were sharing the "taxi" with at least eight other passengers.

"So this is what it feels like to go out with a guy who's not hopelessly closeted," I said to myself. After months of Shane and all of his issues, I'd forgotten what it felt like to kiss someone you were really into in public, straight onlookers be damned. When we returned to my room at Copa, we fell asleep the way we woke up the following morning, hot and unbothered by clothing.

That Shane didn't dominate my thoughts the way he normally did during my trysts with other guys was telling, but by the time I departed Pattaya for Koh Samet the morning after my morning after with Alan, Shane was once again the captain of my heart and foremost in my thoughts. When I returned to Pattaya for two more days after my *koh*-hopping adventure, I didn't even go by Copa to see Alan. I was terrified that this time I wouldn't be able get Shane out of my head — or that I would . . . again. I wasn't sure which outcome was less desirable.

And I wanted to leave the takeaway portion of my fling

with Alan intact: He would go down as one of my favorite memories in Thailand, unsullied by my trying to make it more than it was. But it was good to know that if I changed my mind, I'd know exactly where to find him.

Goodbye, Stranger

One Friday morning in November, Shane and I arrived at yet another parting of ways, in true twenty-first-century style: on Facebook. This time, goodbye was different than it ever had been before. He wasn't going off to class, and I wasn't getting on an airplane. He was still in Melbourne, and I was still in Bangkok, and goodbye didn't mean "See you soon" or "Talk to you later" or "Until tomorrow" or "Take care." This time, goodbye was forever.

What a long, strange trip it had been: thirteen months of wildly inconsistent behavior, hot and cold, like that guy in Katy Perry's best song. Would he be cruel or kind today, love me or loathe me, pay attention or pretend that I didn't exist?

I can't say that I didn't see the breakup coming; even without my glasses, it was visible from miles away. Relationships are hard enough as it is and even more so when they are conducted mostly from the discomfort of your own homes on different continents. It didn't help that I was dealing with someone who was uncommunicative by nature and generally didn't talk in more than three sentences at a time unless he was drunk or lashing out in anger.

I was still sort of reeling from the shock that he had said "I love you" first. Considering his taciturn nature, those were the last words I had ever expected to hear him say — or, rather, text — before I did. He'd repeat them to my face numerous times over the course of the next two months, sober and unprompted. But by November, there were no more "I love yous," just mostly silence.

It was momentarily broken during our final confrontation. Terrible things were said —written — by both of us. I called him cruel and told him that I wanted him out of my life for good. He suggested that I was needy and that I was holding him back. I carefully considered his criticisms and wondered if he had a point.

I decided that they were the mad ramblings of someone who was grasping at straws. How could someone like me, someone with such a fierce independent streak, someone who was almost always a party of one, someone who had spent the five previous years living alone on three continents so far from home, possibly be needy? Would a needy person have left Shane to venture into yet another great unknown? Clingy had never been my thing. OK, I was a bit of a cuddler, but I'd never try to hold anyone's hand as we walked down the street. I rarely had anyone around to cling to, and that was mostly by choice.

I never made any demands on Shane or his time. For the four months that we both were living in Melbourne, we saw each other only a few times a week, and I never pushed for anything more. I had always thrived on and in solitude, so daily togetherness didn't appeal to me. I was OK seeing him two or three times a week as long as we talked every day, which was how I'd approached all of my previous romantic relationships. Sometimes it was nice to fall asleep and wake up with arms around me, but as a lifelong insomniac, I rarely slept like a baby, with or without a lover by my side. And the morning after, although I was usually sad to see Shane leave (a first for me when sleepovers were concerned), I never dreaded being alone again.

As a boyfriend, I generally hated meeting the parents, and I wasn't terribly interested in bonding with the friends. This might not have been conducive to having the healthiest relationships, but if you wanted to spend most of your time with your friends and family (without me tagging along), focus on university and hide in the closet, I had the perfect deal for you. "No wonder you're alone," Shane offered as one of his parting shots, referring to my insular ways while contradicting his claim that I was needy. He'd always characterized himself as being too much of a loner for love. I wondered if he had been looking in the mirror when he'd written that: "No wonder *you're* alone."

For all of my own insistence on having plenty of alone time, daily communication was a must for me, even if it was just a brief phone call, a text message or an email saying, "I'm thinking of you." He and I were generally good at that when I was in Melbourne, although he'd go through those cold snaps every other week, those several-day periods when he would respond to me like the most casual acquaintance, or shut me out completely. It hurt, and our arguments usually stemmed from what I interpreted as indifference on his part. Maybe he perceived my desire to have open lines of communication and express ourselves openly and without fear as neediness.

Several weeks earlier, during our penultimate blowout, he'd blamed his lack of boyfriend etiquette on the fact that he didn't really know how to be in love. He'd always been a lone ranger and suddenly, he was forced to feel, to be lonely when I wasn't around. He wasn't sure how to deal with that.

He also had no idea how to keep me, and he hadn't for some time. Shortly after I moved to Melbourne, when peace had been restored following one of our standoffs, he told me about a dream he had in which I was living with someone else, a man closer to my own age, one who was handsome, successful and out of the closet. I was happy: I had everything I deserved, most importantly a man who wasn't always disappointing me, which is what Shane felt he was constantly doing, though not intentionally. We were never quite the same after that dream, which set up the dramatic unfolding of our relationship. It was like Shane was now certain he'd end up losing me, and through his actions (or lack thereof) turned it into a self-fulfilling prophecy.

My extended time in Asia — that one-month trip that turned into a six-month one — should have been the perfect setup for Shane, someone who hated neediness and didn't want to be held back by romance. For months, he'd said he didn't have a problem with it, but near the bitter end, in his usual roundabout way, he finally admitted that he did. I got that. I understood why he might have felt that I had abandoned him. But it was less the abandonment that bothered him than that it bothered him as much as it did.

If only he'd tried a little empathy. I'd spent four months in Melbourne looking for a job with no success. I had a number of freelance offers, from magazines and even from the University of Melbourne, where I would have taught journalism courses on a guest-lecturer basis, but without a work visa I couldn't freelance for any Australian-based organizations. And Shane wasn't about to propose marriage, a move that would have solved my visa problem. Not that I would have accepted. Before I went to Asia, my plan had been to go to Sydney — the publishing capital of Australia — in hopes that being there would make the job hunt easier.

Then one Saturday evening during a visit from a friend who had just returned from Singapore and was about to go to Bangkok on holiday, Southeast Asia began to look like the best and the cheapest of every possible world. By the following morning, I'd booked my ridiculously inexpensive round-trip flight on Jetstar and reserved a four-star $36-a-night hotel for my first three nights. I was leaving in a week and a half.

I'd only be gone for one month, but it was a good way to put some distance between myself and the place I'd come to associate so much with failure, while gaining some new perspective. My relationship wasn't working either. I figured that if I spent time away from Shane in new surroundings, those regular blasts of coldness wouldn't hurt so much.

I ended up staying largely because of economics. Melbourne was like a money pit compared to Bangkok, so it made sense for me to live in Bangkok while waiting to be "discovered" by a potential employer in Australia. I also could freelance for Australian publications while I was outside of the country. To my knowledge, the guy who claimed to love me had never really considered how challenging moving to Australia — something I had decided to do before we'd met thirteen months earlier — had been for me. I tried to explain it to him, but he'd stare at me blankly, like he was wishing I'd change the subject.

In the end, I think he was resentful and angry with me for staying away. We'd communicated only sporadically during the previous four months. There had been a few clumsy attempts at regular Facebook chats early on, but he didn't speak or write in paragraphs unless he was angry. His three-word responses frustrated me, so I never instigated our Facebook conversations, a lack of effort that, as I found out during our breakup exchange, hadn't gone unnoticed by him.

Maybe he felt he had to punish me, and I loaded his pistol for him. One week before we broke up, I had a conversation with my brother Alexi, who encouraged me to be more forthcoming with Shane about my feelings, so I sent an email in which I told Shane how much I missed him. I was testing the waters, seeing if it was time for me to go back to Melbourne and finally attempt to have an exclusive relationship with him.

For an entire week, he ignored it, ignored me, until I sent a follow-up.

Me: *Hi, Shane. I sent you a very nice email a week ago, and you never even bothered to respond. I won't be bothering you anymore. Jeremy*

Him: :(

Me: *Typical response.*

With those two words, I opened up the floodgates. He shot back full of fire and ire, dropping those allegations that I was needy and holding him back. He made my initial email, the one he'd ignored, seem so trivial, like the blabbering of a lovesick fool: What had there been to respond to? If being hurt by that made me a needy person, then the shoe fit. Wouldn't anyone — both the needy and the secure — have felt the sting of unanswered emails and text messages to someone they loved who claimed to love them back?

"I wasn't in the right headspace to respond" was how he explained his dead silence, several emails later. For an entire week? He couldn't snap out of his malaise long enough to compose a two-sentence response: "Thinking about you. Miss you, too"? It wouldn't have been the best that he could do, but it would have been so much better than doing nothing. He seemed to be genuinely surprised that I was so hurt and offended. "And to think, all of this just because I didn't answer an email in which you compared me to a pillow," he wrote near the end of his final email to me.

Some guys would be touched that an absent lover would go to sleep hugging a pillow, pretending that it was him. For Shane, it was fodder for future ammunition.

As for my holding him back, I wasn't sure how that was even possible, considering that we'd spent nine of the thirteen months we'd known each other on separate continents. Even when I was in Melbourne, he was free to do what he wanted to do. I probably would have happily accepted more than the normal two or three dates a week that I usually required, but he had a lot going on, and I'd never done clingy. Desperation looked as horrible on me as baseball caps did.

Perhaps it wasn't me but rather his feelings for me that were holding him back. Maybe he didn't want to deal with the messiness of love and romance. He wanted to be the lone ranger. He was about to get his wish. But he was still going to have to deal with those feelings. Just because I was exiting his life didn't mean he wouldn't have to live with all of those untidy emotions he'd been trying so hard to push under the bed.

In the end, I didn't want harsh words to be the last ones Shane heard from me, so I sent him a cordial postmortem email in which I explained my actions since leaving Melbourne and defended myself against his accusations of neediness (that one had stung the most), leaving the door open for further communication. I didn't know whether he would use the door. He was still trapped in the closet, so opening doors and walking through them wasn't his strength.

I wasn't sure if there was a chance of reconciliation, and I felt strangely ambivalent about the possibility. I was actually looking forward to going back to being me, someone who wasn't so emotionally crippled by uncertainty and insecurity. By the end of the day, Shane had defriended me on Facebook, a move that said a lot more than he had over the course of four months. It was the 2011 version of romantic finality. Of course, there was always the option of refriending. It wouldn't have been the first time for him and me.

But in that moment, I was pretty much over it. If this wasn't the end of our wild and crazy ride, I knew that it should be. It was time to get off. After so many months of being tossed and turned with my insides spinning around, I was ready to embrace the peaceful easy feeling that comes from not being entangled by a guy.

At least until the next one came along.

There's Nothing Cold as Ashes After the Fire Is Gone

I spent the weekend after the breakup trying to climb up from the emotional wreckage. I covered pretty much the entire spectrum of feelings — sadness, anger, relief, confusion, love, lust, loss, hate, hope, etc. — sometimes all in the space of five minutes.

And I still felt terrible.

Some of my friends and family offered their support and their unique takes on the situation, and a lot of what they said was revelatory. Lori mentioned how the modern age has brought a whole new level of stress to relationships. Because we're all so plugged-in, always available via emails, texts, iPhone apps and so on, nonresponses seem not only negligent but hostile, too. Back in the good old days, when reaching out and touching someone meant actually doing just that, or at least picking up a telephone, if the person didn't get right back to you, you could comfort yourself with easy excuses: Maybe they were too busy to call, or perhaps they hadn't checked their voice mail. Now it's not so easy to rationalize the silent treatment.

It was so telling that within minutes, Shane had answered my email commenting on his nonresponse to the one from a week before. And in true modern twenty-two-year-old style, he'd done so in less than three characters, and without bothering to type any actual words. I couldn't get that pathetic, flippant :(out of my head.

The next time I got involved with someone, I decided, there would be no exchanging email addresses and no Facebook friending. Oh, and texting would be kept to a minimum. It would force us to communicate in real time the way people did when conversations took on the form of actual paragraphs — spoken ones — and not silly acronyms and symbols. An actual laugh sounds so much nicer than LOL looks! Had Shane and I hashed things out on the telephone rather than on Facebook, the altercation might have ended with the sound of real laughter and "I love you." For that, I accepted part of the blame. Instead of expressing my disappointment via email, I should have called.

Lori also understood Shane's pain. "But he's so young. And you've left him for so many months!" she wrote in an email to me. I couldn't argue with that. I owned the role that my living and working (or more accurately, *not* working) situation played in the difficulty of our relationship, and in my final email to him, I apologized for it.

In the past, Shane always had been good about saying he was sorry, owning his own misdeeds and acknowledging the role he played in our blowouts. But not this time. He didn't seem to realize or he simply didn't care how hurtful not responding to my first email had been. I kept telling myself that deep down he must have known how wrong he'd been and he was kicking himself for his negligence. Or not. I knew

I might not hear from him again, and I had to find a way to be OK with that.

Devarni said that whenever his name popped into my head, I should send it on its way. I knew I was as likely to be that resolute in my recovery as I was to have a healthy romantic relationship with another closeted guy in his early twenties. Being a writer, I would no doubt spend months writing about and analyzing to death every detail of Shane vs. Jeremy. But I promised myself not to become like Carrie Bradshaw after she broke up with Big the first time on *Sex and the City,* when her friends had to stage an intervention.

Alexi said, Don't dream it's over. He suggested that when I return to Melbourne, I meet up with Shane, take his hands in mine and look into his eyes. That would tell me everything I needed to know.

Too bad he'd be wearing sunglasses.

Like a Drug

I always prided myself on not having an addictive personality, but three weeks after I ended things with Shane, I think I understood how bad addicts had it. I was still hooked — on Shane, on love, on the security of knowing that someone was waiting for me back in Australia, although that was no longer the case.

Instead of climbing to higher emotional ground, I felt as if I was plunging backwards into an abyss of gloom. And to think, one week earlier, I had been worried that I was getting over everything too quickly: Was the worst already behind me? Ambivalence was beginning to feel like indifference, and part of me didn't want it to because I didn't think it was healthy to rush through the grieving process. But my recovery didn't last long. One day I was falling out of love, onward and upward, the next I was relapsing, falling again, several steps, or twelve, in the other direction.

Had I done the right thing? Was there any getting over Shane? In spite of what we both had written in that final exchange, could we still have a future together?

Mark, a forty-three-year-old guy from Massachusetts whom I met at DJ Station and promptly brought home with me, said no. He'd recently broken up with his own early-twentysomething boyfriend, so he'd been there. He said that Shane didn't understand where I was coming from because he couldn't, not due to his age but due to his nature. One day he might have an epiphany and realize that if you love someone, you don't ignore an email from him for an entire week. But I couldn't help him along the road to maturity. He was going to have to negotiate it on his own.

Should I have reached out to Shane anyway? During my weaker moments, I wanted to pick up the phone and maybe the pieces, too. I wanted to know if he was OK, if he missed me, if he still loved me, if he ever really did.

"No, you shouldn't contact him. It's over." That was Mark's final answer just before he left to catch a flight to Sydney.

Why couldn't I accept an end that I had decided on? It's not as if things were that much different than before Shane and I had broken up. Even when I was in Melbourne, our relationship had played out mostly in my mind, which was constantly replaying text messages, IMs, days of silence — moments in times in which we'd been physically apart. It was easier to remember the hours I'd spent agonizing over Shane in my head than anything we'd actually done together. So why was it so much harder to untangle myself emotionally from this relationship than past ones that involved far more quality time spent in the same room? Was it because I was mourning a love I never had? Did that make it even harder to let go?

That week after we broke up, I asked my friend Dov to contact Shane and arrange to pick up a bag of my things from him. I secretly hoped the exchange wouldn't happen. The stuff Shane had been keeping for me while I was in Asia was my last connection to him, the only reason left why I had to see him when I got back to Melbourne. I also was being ridiculously insecure: What if Shane and Dov hit it off? What if I logged on to Facebook the next day and saw that they had become friends? What if they began dating? What if they fell in love?

 Shane's birthday was on my mind, too. He'd be twenty-three in two weeks. Should I call him to wish him a happy birthday? After the way he had taken care of me on my birthday, making me dinner the night before and spending most of the day with me, did I owe him at least a "Thinking about you" email?

 But then, he hadn't responded to that final email I'd sent him. Did that mean he was through with me? Maybe he never received it. Facebook wasn't always so dependable, especially when you were communicating with non-friends. Maybe the email went to some strange inbox that he never checked. I had one labeled *Other* where I was always finding unread emails weeks after I'd received them. I was pretty sure he wasn't reading my blog, so maybe the most recent words he'd read from me were still the ones telling him that I didn't want anything more to do with him.

 One night I had a dream about Shane — actually, two of them. I wasn't sure where we were, and the storyline was pretty fuzzy when I woke up. But I did remember that we were together again. It felt like we'd never said goodbye. I was so disappointed when I woke up alone. I'd fallen asleep with him on my mind because of GetUp's beautiful new pro—gay marriage ad that was circulating online in Australia. The main character could have been Shane's twin brother. I wanted to send him the link to the video. Maybe he'd recognize himself in his near-doppelgänger, who got on his knees and proposed to his boyfriend in front of family and friends at the end, and it would shove him out of the closet once and for all. Maybe he'd finally respond to that final email.

I'd stopped waiting to hear back from him. I'd stopped expecting him to drunk-dial me in the middle of the night. Now that I was out of hope, if not out of love, and had no expectations, maybe Shane would surprise me. Maybe he'd call me up, sober, and tell me how sorry he was for ignoring that first email, the one that started the whole mess, and how he didn't mean all of those cruel things he'd written, and how he really wanted us to work. Maybe we'd finally have "the talk" and try to have a real relationship. I was resigned to our romantic fate and in denial at the same time.

As usual, I found solace in song. One night I was singing "You Won't Forget Me" by La Bouche, with Shane as my imaginary target audience. Maybe there ain't no getting over me either, I thought, echoing Ronnie Milsap in my mind. Maybe he was a total mess, wracked with guilt and grief, dreaming of me (Depeche Mode!) and wondering if there was a way to win me back.

I hoped so. Not only because misery loves company but also because we'd have something very powerful in common, our despair, and wouldn't common ground have been the perfect foundation on which to reconnect and rebuild a relationship? Wasn't that the idea behind grief sex? But where words — or, rather, a lack of them — used to get in the way, now it was pride. "Love is stronger than pride," Sade sang on one of her best songs. Not necessarily.

She also sang "It's only love that gets you through." Wrong again. Sometimes it took a shot of whiskey and a shot of denial to get me through, if only for one night. But I figured I'd stay away from Jack Daniel for a while. I could only deal with one addiction at a time.

The Last Goodbye?

When I saw Shane for the first time in seven months, our reunion in Melbourne was a medley of mixed emotional and mental states: confusion, clarity, fear, acceptance, disappointment, relief, tension and awkwardness . . . so much awkwardness.

We'd barely spoken since breaking up in November, so I wasn't expecting sidesplitting conversation or breezy banter on a brutally scorching summer afternoon in February. But I didn't think it would feel so much like a first date with a total stranger. I probably would have been more comfortable squirming in a dentist's chair with my mouth stretched open, listening to the scary buzzing of a pointy drilling machine.

The gain from this particular pain, though, had nothing to do with nicer teeth or a buff body. When it was over, I felt as if I'd arrived at that elusive state of closure. Now, there was a word I'd always sort of hated — but not by the end of my meeting with Shane. For the first time, I felt like I fully understood it, and I said so when I updated my Facebook status immediately after returning home:

Closure is a very underrated thing. Or maybe it's just that it's not overrated. At any rate, thank God for it.

But I'm getting ahead of myself. Let's backtrack to shortly after 1 p.m.

Shane had invited me to a late lunch at the last minute. Designated time and place: 2:30 p.m. at Burger Edge, one of our old local haunts, only one block from where I was living on St. Kilda Road in Melbourne. He was going to give me back the things he had been holding for me: my stash of Kiehl's products and other assorted toiletries, the red and gray Armani hoodie he loved (the one I'd worn the night he cooked my birthday dinner), CDs and DVDs, including one called *Great Things About Being . . . Queer*. Shane was slowly beginning to come out to friends and family members, and before watching *Great Things*, a Bravo program I had appeared on as a commentator/expert, he'd taken one look at the DVD case and read it as a private message from me to him.

Presumably, we'd also gain that closure. It was neither his word nor mine, but things between us needed to end on a harmonious note that didn't sound like fingers furiously tapping a laptop keyboard. I accepted, though I had eaten shortly before his email arrived.

I decided that I'd wear what I had on, which meant that I looked like I had just rolled out of bed, having actually taken a nap in the green Siouxsie and the Banshees T-shirt and khaki shorts I'd be wearing. I didn't shower, and I didn't floss and brush my teeth, as I generally did before meeting up with any handsome guy. Who needed the possibility of sex clouding my good judgment?

Shane arrived about thirty minutes late — though he did send several apologetic emails en route — and when I saw him across the street, I wanted to run to him in slow motion.

He looked surfer-hot in a blue Topshop T-shirt and beige shorts that showed off his tan muscular legs, with his dark blond hair tousled to the left. As he told me within seconds of sitting down, he was doing great, too, "really, really great": He had a new apartment and new roommates in Balaclava, one neighborhood east of St. Kilda, where we'd both been living when we met. There were job prospects as a store designer for Adidas or Ben Sherman in Sydney after his graduation, six months away. Most momentously, he'd come out to his big brother Kaley, who'd been supportive and accepting. I was happy for him in that clap-when-the-Oscar-goes-to-someone-else way, but sad for me because it meant that life really did go on without me.

Did he *look* happy? Not particularly, but then he rarely ever did. He wore his sunglasses the entire time, so I couldn't get a read on what was really going on inside. Though we were seated alfresco and the sun *was* shining brightly, I knew the shades were meant to convey my-life-so-doesn't-suck-without-you insouciance. At one point, I considered asking him to remove them so that I could see his eyes, but I didn't. I was afraid of what I might see, and I didn't want him to think I cared. We were both playing it too cool.

They say the couple that belongs together is the couple that's comfortable being quiet together. Shane and I had always been one of those couples, but that was usually when we were in cuddling mode. They also say true friends can go without seeing each other for months, or years even, and when they reunite, it's like they just saw each other yesterday. The conversation picks up right where they left it. Shane and I had too much baggage for that, and our last conversation had been like a landmine loaded with explosive potential. If it had contained a warning label, it would have read *Do not touch!* So we proceeded with extreme caution, not the best mental environment for scintillating conversation.

That afternoon in front of Burger Edge as we danced around flammable topics, I arrived at a difficult realization about Shane and me: Take away sex, or the possibility of it, and our connection was frayed. Sure, we were more than physical. There was chemistry, and genuine emotion and affection. What we lacked, what we'd always lacked, was an intellectual bond, the easy rapport of friends.

I thought about those older couples I sometimes saw in restaurants eating in what appeared to be tense silence (bodies rigid, chewing slow and deliberate, eyes avoiding contact with the ones across from them), not the sort of comfortable silence that comes from a deep, ongoing yearslong bond. I always figured that they'd never had anything in common, or that they'd run out of things to talk about. Shane and I had so much to discuss that afternoon, but we were carefully sidestepping the important stuff in favor of dwelling on the meaningless minutiae of our lives over the previous half year.

Sitting beside me eating his cheeseburger, Shane reminded me of Paris (the city, not the Trojan), beautiful but oh-so-boring. If only we had been in a café overlooking the Seine, or at the Louvre, standing in front of the Mona Lisa. At least then when I'd divert my gaze from him, I would have had a perfect excuse for it, not that I simply couldn't bear to look into those black circles (his sunglasses) for one second longer.

Shane was one of those people who rarely dug deep — at least, not with me. He began every conversation with pretty much the same question: What's going on? That is what made talking to him about intangible things like feelings so frustrating. He was most comfortable recounting events, what was happening in his life, or in someone else's. And he went on and on about his life — his internship, what his friends were doing or about to do and the movie he had seen the night before, *Requiem for a Dream* (only how "awesome" it was, not any of the psychological themes it explored). I'd never heard him talk so much.

But he didn't have much to say about anything I said that wasn't about him. So I offered him professional encouragement, asked him about his short-term plans and aspirations, anything to keep the focus on Shane. The only thing I mentioned about my life that seemed to make any real impression on him was that beginning the following month, I would be writing two columns for a magazine in Bangkok. When I talked about the writing I'd been doing over the past seven months, which had been such a key component of my life, he seemed to be shrugging on the inside, maybe even stifling a yawn. For such a talented, creative person, he'd always been strangely unwilling or unable to talk about the creative process, his own, or anyone else's.

He did throw in a few polite questions about me, but his intent seemed to be more to restart the conversation during a weird pause than to collect crucial intel: How was my job search going? What did I like most about my time in Asia? (Clearly he wasn't reading my blog, or he wouldn't have had to ask.) What was I going to do now?

"Do you mean *now* now, or now as in, What am I going to do with the rest of my life?"

He didn't really know. "I guess it's just something people ask." So he'd asked it, which was so typical.

In lieu of answering, I started babbling about the internal journey I'd been on in Southeast Asia, and how it had changed my outlook and my life. I was calmer, more optimistic (though somewhat guardedly), more in the moment. Was he still listening? I felt like I was looking into the sunglasses of a disinterested and uninterested stranger. Maybe behind the dark lenses there was some spark, a flicker of feeling, but all I could see were those two black circles staring back at me. After I was finished with my rambling monologue about what I'd done last summer in Asia, he was silent. I wasn't even sure if he was still awake.

We never did get around to talking about us that day. We

didn't discuss what went wrong or offer any sort of belated post-breakup commentary. I wanted to say *something,* but I was afraid that Shane no longer cared. Maybe he figured that everything that needed to be said had already been said on Facebook.

Sometime around 4 p.m., Shane announced that he should leave. I hadn't eaten anything, so I'd been ready to flee the scene as soon as he'd arrived and I'd gotten my things from him. I probably should have, but how rude would that have been? I figured the least I could do was let *him* decide how we'd leave things this time. He started to mumble something about being glad that we could have this last conversation and held out his hand. I hugged him instead.

"Good luck with everything," he said. Finality.

"Have fun at your friend's party tonight," I said. I wanted to leave the door ajar just a little, although I knew that I'd slammed it shut when I broke up with him in November.

I left the encounter feeling sad yet strangely elated. Sad because life goes on; elated for the same reason. I knew it was over, and unlike Morrissey in the great Smiths song "I Know It's Over," I would try not to cling, even though I still loved him, and I was pretty certain that part of me always would.

As we walked away from each other, I didn't glance back. I knew he was leaving my life for good. I couldn't bear to look.

The Greatest Show on Earth

I may have lost the guy, but in the end, I gained so much more. Not because it's better to have loved and lost (I'm still not entirely convinced that's true), but because my nearly six years of living in self-imposed exile from New York City wasn't just about a boy.

I couldn't pinpoint the precise epiphanic moment when I finally realized how far I'd come — from materialistic, career-obsessed, slightly jaded New Yorker to a happily unemployed citizen of the world who could fit everything he owned into two suitcases and spend hours marveling at the wonder of an elephant. It was somewhere between Melbourne and Asia, the second time. I was still thinking about Shane every day. I never completely got over him, or gave up hope, which on some days felt more like a hunch, that one day we might be together again.

Despite Shane's ongoing presence in my emotional life, I was doing something I wouldn't have dreamed was possible one year earlier: I was living in the moment. During my first six months in Southeast Asia, I'd learned how to travel through life without a road map. It was the first time that I'd ever allowed myself to live free of an agenda, to make game-time decisions, to be ready to pick up and leave at a moment's notice or to stay longer than intended. If I made any plans during my time in Asia, I always wrote them down in pencil.

Home became a state of mind; it was where my mind was. I began unpacking and decorating it in that minimalist style I loved so much. A clear mind equaled a clear vision, though not in the sense of what I could actually see. I had no idea what lay ahead on my road less traveled — life's a dance, and I guess you could say I was dancing in the dark — and I'd tossed my map out the window. I couldn't see what was in front of me, but I'd never experienced the passing scenery, the view from the side windows, with such clarity.

Once, after I'd returned to Melbourne, a few weeks before I said goodbye to Shane for the last time, I even stopped to smell the flowers — literally. Heartbroken as I was following our final encounter, I didn't take my eyes off the world, not in Melbourne, not in Bangkok, when I returned one month later, and especially not in Chiang Mai, two months after that. There was so much natural beauty to stop for in Chiang Mai. You knew you'd been thoroughly entertained when, during the course of an afternoon, you'd seen elephants score soccer goals, shoot hoops and paint landscapes on a canvas with their trunks. The monkey business was no less impressive. One of them lifted weights, another flexed his numerical skills (someone in the audience of five would pick a number — say, seven — and the monkey would pick the card with 7 on it, even when it was facedown), and yet another, "Monkey Jordan," shot hoops and made them all except for one. (What was it with animals in Thailand and basketball, anyway?)

The animal shows made me cheer and cringe. The pets appeared to be happy and eager to show off how smart they were, but something about it seemed off, like their primary purpose in life was to entertain *us*. The chains around the monkeys' necks didn't help. They only highlighted the fact that they were the prisoners and the Thai people who ran the conservation/training centers, as loving and gentle as they might have been, were their captors.

I tried to forget all of this as Lori and I sat on Oz, the beautiful twenty-year-old elephant who took us on an hourlong ride up and down the mountains of Chiang Mai. We sat in a compartment chained around Oz's body while Deng, a handsome twenty-two-year-old local who had been Oz's daily companion for four years, sat on his back, riding him like one would ride a horse and assuring us that despite our weight on Oz's back, the elephant was not only comfortable but happy, too.

Aside from the part when they played around in the water, the fierce felines that Lori spent an hour petting at the tiger kingdom had far less taxing things to do than entertain us. For the most part, they lounged around their living rooms, waiting to receive guests, who would pay from 420 baht (or $14) to nearly 2,000 ($66) for the honor of petting them. (One of the workers, an American expat, told Lori, they were all younger than two years old, the age when they became too unpredictable not to pose a threat to interlopers.)

By the time we left, Lori was tearing up over everything

she'd seen. My eyes were dry, but I was a little choked up, too. Not over the animals, though. As touching as they were, they weren't the main cause of my emotional state. It was the locals who worked with them and all the others we'd encountered in Chiang Mai: Danny, the guy who had spent all day driving us around from attraction to attraction in the van; the precious Thai children we'd seen throughout the day. I couldn't believe how beautiful and well behaved they were, like perfect little angels.

I'd been living in Thailand for the better part of ten months, and for the first time since my arrival, in Chiang Mai I felt as if I finally got the Thai people. I'd known that they were kind, friendly and gentle, but this was the first time I truly realized how content they were, how proud they were of their heritage and their country.

Here was Deng, a twenty-two-year-old who lived to take care of an elephant. His home was on the grounds of the conservation center, with his elephant charge, in conditions that I assumed were somewhere around half a star, making 4,000 baht (roughly $130) a month. He hadn't had a day off in four years, yet he seemed like one of the happiest people I'd met in a long time. He had no girlfriend (or boyfriend), and his parents lived far away in Myanmar, yet I didn't get the impression that he felt alone at all. Even if he hadn't been so friendly and gorgeous, he still would have been unforgettable.

As I listened to Deng try to tell us in English what life was like for him and Oz, I thought of the lives I'd left behind, in the U.S., in Argentina, in Australia, even in Bangkok. I thought about the people in all of those places, the ones who were so obsessed with making money and spending it. They were looking for happiness on the job, in accumulating wealth, in material possessions, in overpriced homes, in picking up strangers in crowded bars and clubs, in chasing celebrity (and celebrities). So few of them seemed truly happy to me.

Mikey, the hyperactive two-year-old monkey circling the small raised platform, barely stopping to catch his breath, and Sonny, the four-year-old who knew exactly what to do when he was told to "kiss" visitors, seemed more full of joie de vivre than any Western human being I could remember having seen in years.

And all they had were the chains around their necks.

IV. Don't Touch Me There!

Keep Your Hands to Yourself

One day I came across a missed email from my Facebook friend and former colleague Karen. She'd sent it to me a few days before I left Melbourne for Southeast Asia, and in it, she'd issued a stern warning: "Do not, under any circumstances, set foot in Cambodia. You can only enjoy it from the comfort of five-star accommodations, and the men are 'sexual predators.'"

It was interesting to read her take on the place in hindsight, especially since Cambodia had ended up being my favorite stop on my summer tour of Southeast Asia. Britney Spears' concurrent Femme Fatale Tour may not have made it to Phnom Penh or Siem Reap, but I was glad mine did. I was thankful that I'd somehow overlooked Karen's message until it was too late, but I had to admit, she had a point or two.

The first part certainly turned out to be true. At my age, I could no longer settle for dingy *pensiones* like the ones I'd called temporary home in Madrid, Barcelona and throughout the South of France when I first visited Europe in 1993 at twenty-four, and hostels where you're assigned one of six rock-hard single-person cots in a room simply wouldn't do. I'd never actually stayed in a place with shared sleeping quarters, but I'd heard a lot about the experience, none of it enticing.

Although I did come dangerously close to having to sleep with a stranger on top of me in a hostel in Budapest in 1996,

I lucked out and snagged the last available private room. It was worth the extra cost because the wrong accommodations can ruin just about any city. And if I could get a luxury room for less than $50 a night, as I did at Siem Reap's Tara Angkor Hotel (which was technically a four-star joint with five-star trappings, like the most decadent breakfast buffet, featuring dinnertime options that I normally wouldn't have dreamed of devouring first thing in the morning), why not splurge?

Unfortunately, Karen was right about the local men, too — at least, many of the ones I encountered after sundown. They couldn't have been nicer to me, but they sure liked to use their hands. It's one thing to direct crude commentary to hot passersby. As I always said, "Say it, just don't spray it," and "You can look, but don't touch me there." In Cambodia, though, the men liked to watch — and touch.

Being male, I could hold my own, but to all the single ladies considering visiting Cambodia, beware. Proceed with caution when venturing out at night. Put a ring on it (to help ward off unwanted advances), and grab a friend. While I didn't actually notice any heterosexual behavior that was worse than what I regularly used to see in Buenos Aires (men on the sidewalk, by the bar, on the dance floor, ogling every woman who walked by), I'd never had so many touchy-feely encounters outside of a gay bar. I could only imagine what my female fellow travelers must have been going through when I wasn't paying attention.

There were no women at Linga Bar in Siem Reap, and if there had been, they would have been a lot safer in that gay bar than I was in any of the straight ones. As I sipped my primary-colored drink, I tried to avoid eye contact with the kid whose hungry eyes were burning holes into me from across the table. His English was barely intelligible, so after a while, I gave up trying to communicate with him and just prayed that he'd get the message and go away. For a long time, he didn't. He begged me to take him back to my hotel room. He wouldn't try anything, just give me a massage. "How old can this child be?" I asked myself, placing his age somewhere around barely legal.

I decided to ask. "How old are you?"

"Thirty-two." He had to be kidding. I said he didn't look a day over sixteen.

After some cajoling, I got the truth out of him. He was twenty-one. I wouldn't reveal my age, but I did tell him that I was old enough to know better than to mess with boys his age, which, given my track record since I'd left New York City for Buenos Aires, was pretty laughable. It's not that he was unattractive (although he was a little too much on the dainty and petite side). I just couldn't deal with the way he was staring at me, like he couldn't wait to feast on my meat. At least he kept his hands to himself.

I didn't believe it was possible to have such a great time in a "gay-friendly" straight bar until another local swinger who'd also struck out trying to hit on me continued his courtship by taking me to Temple Bar a little later. Considering how empty Linga Bar and the other gay hole in the wall he'd taken me to had been on a Friday night, I was kind of surprised to see Temple Bar so full of tourists, expats and Cambodians. I met people from all over the world — from Ireland, from Amsterdam, from Scandinavia, from pretty much every corner of Europe. There was even one beautiful black girl from Saint Martin, the Caribbean island where my dad is from. How often did *that* happen? Right: never.

   The booze was cheap (pitchers of beer, or of whiskey and Coke, for $2.75!), and so were the thrills. The local boys' hands were all over, everywhere, on everything. Had I blacked out and woken up on the dance floor at Plop! in Buenos Aires? Every time I turned around, I seemed to be swatting away another pair.

   Some wanted to check out the bull tattoo on my right arm. Others wanted to compare their hands to the animated one on my T-shirt. Several wanted to see what was going on just south of halfway down. "Is it true what they say about black men?" Here we go again, and again, and again. In general, I hated to be touched by strangers, but whiskey had a way of removing my inhibitions and my boundaries. At some point, I stopped pulling away and just went with it.

   I looked around the room filled with Asians, white Europeans and one black girl. Was I getting so much attention because guys like me were such a rarity in that part of the world and people wanted to see if it was true what they say about black men? That always had been my assumption while I was living in Buenos Aires and Australia, but in Cambodia, my rapt audience wasn't limited to gay men and straight women, and few people seemed content to simply stop, stare and maybe make a clumsy attempt at launching a conversation.

    I saw white guys getting looks in Temple Bar, but they didn't seem to come from a range of people that covered every demographic, gender and sexual persuasion, and as far as I could tell, none of the good-looking white men (and there were quite a few crowding my line of vision) had to defend their personal space. If Ryan Gosling weren't famous and he walked into Temple Bar, surely people would look, but would they touch as well?

    When I returned to Bangkok a few days later, I was more aware of how people were responding to me in Southeast Asia. At DJ Station, it wasn't so much different than it had been in Temple Bar. Neither was my pattern of rejection — though, thankfully, none of the reactions were ever as ruthless as Marcelo's had been at KM Zero in Buenos Aires a few years earlier. Inviting yourself back to my hotel within one minute of meeting me was not the best way to get past the velvet rope into my VIP area. Neither was a cupped hand to the crotch. But DJ Station was a gay bar. You went there expecting unsolicited advances, some more extreme than others.

Unfortunately, the two Cambodians I ran into in DJ Station the following weekend (one of whom was the one who'd taken me to Temple Bar) didn't learn anything in Siem Reap, where they both had been roundly rejected after numerous crotch-grabbing attempts. There they were, near the entrance as I arrived, waving with one hand and reaching for my crotch with the other. I smiled and tried to be polite, which was hard when all I wanted to do was slug them. I'd dealt with forward club patrons before — at Plop! and Ambar la Fox in Buenos Aires, they sometimes literally threw themselves at me to get the attention of *el negro* — but wasn't grabbing a man's crotch in public like walking up to a woman and squeezing her breasts?

I figured the rules of bar conduct were different when you were dealing with men and women. For me, these were cringeworthy but funny stories to laugh about now and tell the grandkids later. If I'd wanted to, I easily could have taken down my overzealous fans. For a woman, who would likely be smaller and weaker than her sexual predator, it must have been a holiday nightmare. The morning after my Temple Bar gropefest, I read a frightening article about several recent cases in which intoxicated women had been raped by taxi drivers in Melbourne and Sydney after passing out in the cabs. Now, there was something that would never happen to me — and God knows a few cabbies, like the tuk-tuk driver who had dropped me off at the Tara Angkor Hotel after Temple Bar, had had the opportunity.

I could deal with random hands on my crotch in the bar if I didn't have to worry about coming to later with some big burly cab driver standing over me, zipping up his trousers. Was that really the sort of thing that women had to live in fear of? It was bad enough when perfect strangers in crowded bars tried to reach out and touch them, but if they made it to last call intact, they still had to worry about remaining that way during the ride home. I used to think that maybe women overreacted to the threat of horny, desperate creeps, but now that I had some small insight into what it felt like for a girl, I wasn't so sure.

No wonder there were always so many of them seeking haven at DJ Station. If anyone was getting touched inappropriately there, it was probably going to be me.

Right Into the Danger Zone

One rainy evening in Bangkok, I had what must qualify as one of my most awkward WTF experiences ever. It was a true Jack Tripper moment, a misunderstanding of epic *Three's Company*—style proportions. If only Janet had been there to talk me out of bumbling, fumbling mode.

It started with a sign — a billboard with a woman in repose, lying on her stomach, looking as relaxed as I wanted to be — in front of the entrance to a massage spa called Oasis. I had an idea. After two near-sleepless nights, during which I was kept awake by worry over alternating pain in my lower back and the upper left quadrant of my stomach (the latter of which may have been all in my mind, thanks to the power of suggestion by a massage therapist in Kuala Lumpur who asked if I suffered from gastric problems after a reflexology treatment), was this the answer? A soothing solution to my insomnia that might possibly even get me blinking again? Instead, what I got was a guarantee of at least another week of sleeplessness, or certainly nightmares, if I was lucky/unlucky enough ever to doze off again.

I was always a bit suspicious of Thai massage spas where the workers tried to lure passersby inside. Although the sexually charged sales pitch of the female employees loitering outside made my warning antennae go up ("Massage? Massage?" in the same suggestive tone I'd heard coming from the lady-boys in the red-light district), I was desperate. I went inside and requested the ninety-minute head/shoulders/back massage for 500 baht ($17). A man led me upstairs and handed me my massage attire.

"Man or woman?" he asked.

I was confused. None of the massage spas I'd gone to in Thailand, Cambodia or Malaysia had ever offered me a choice before. I wasn't in the mood for extreme pain, so I declined the strong arms of a man. I wanted a softer healing touch.

"Woman." Those warning antennae went up again. As the man ran downstairs, I got this feeling of foreboding, like I'd just made the wrong choice. Where was Janet when I needed her?!

Soon after, the female therapist arrived and got to work. She asked all of the boring questions — Where are you from? Are you here on holiday? — and I answered as succinctly as possible to discourage further conversation because my idea of relaxation doesn't involve small talk. Otherwise, the first fifteen minutes or so were uneventful. I barely felt a thing. I didn't want to be holding back tears because of the pain, but she really needed to put a bit more oomph into it. It felt like she was caressing me more than massaging me.

Those warning antennae went up again.

After about twenty minutes, I began to feel uncomfortable lying on my stomach with my head to one side. I worried that after ninety minutes of this, I'd need neck therapy, so I began to shuffle my body around in search of a comfortable position. She suggested I lie on my back.

Warning antennae: Up up up!

But I did as I was told. Ah, much better. Phase two of the massage started off innocently enough, but soon her hands were working their way up and down my thigh, inching closer and closer to my crotch. The signals from those warning antennae were out of control. Should I say something now or wait for the inevitable to happen? Just as I was about to issue a hands-off-the-merchandise policy, she was cupping my crotch with her hand. Then she put her index finger right in the middle of it. I opened my eyes and glared at her.

"Massage?" she asked.

"What the hell are you doing?"

She was pressing it with her finger. "Massage?"

If she'd been dying to ask the question that she'd probably been wondering about from the moment she walked in and saw me lying on the table, the one I'd been asked so often that the challenge now was to come up with creative ways to provide a nonanswer — "Is it true what they say about black men?" — now she wouldn't have to. She'd found out for herself.

"No! I came here for a normal massage, not to be fondled." Didn't she know better than to mess with a brother?

"Oh, you asked for woman, so I thought . . ."

"Yes, I asked for a woman because I wanted someone who

would give me a softer massage. I'm not looking for sex."

I wasn't sure if she was getting what I was saying, so I jumped off the bed and ran downstairs to try to reverse my misfortune. There were other customers, some dressed in business suits, getting foot massages. I wondered if they were in for the full-body treatment.

The man who'd led me upstairs explained that since I'd requested a woman, he'd assumed that I wanted "full" service. He offered to finish what she'd started, hand job not included. Once he got to work, I wished I had heeded my warning antennae and stuck with him in the first place. I could have lived without more personal questions (massage therapists should be seen and felt, not heard), but he worked the knots out of my back with all the force that my torso needed.

He used body oil with eucalyptus-like qualities that soothed my back and made it feel like it was breathing freely for the first time in years. Though I didn't quite get my money's worth, in the end, I was relieved of my physical, if not psychological, tension (here come nightmares!), and I had a funny story to tell my friends.

A sort-of happy ending without a "happy ending."

Love for Sale

I was having yet another five-star-on-a-budget Bangkok lunch, this one in a hospital cafe, of all places, when I heard something that made my jaw drop so far that it nearly landed on my curry chicken and rice. The two French friends of Marc, the Belgian Etihad Airways flight attendant from the night before, were telling me about a special Thai massage — a *naked* Thai massage! — that I just *had* to experience.

Now, I was willing to try everything twice, and I sometimes welcomed extremely awkward situations because they provided excellent storytelling fodder for perking up stalled conversations. But considering how I had felt about the female massage therapist fingering my private parts from outside my shorts several weeks earlier, I wasn't so sure that I was ready to take them off for a nude masseur.

That's not to say I didn't find the concept intriguing, particularly the beginning, which included a lineup of beautiful Thai guys. You got to choose: short or tall, muscular or lean, top or bottom. (Actually, that last one wasn't one of the choices, but it did seem to come up in pretty much every conversation in Bangkok involving gay men.) Once you took your pick, the two of you got undressed and hit the shower. After he soaped you up and rinsed you off — an erotic ablution that was included in the rate (1,300 baht for one hour, or about $43) — the pressing and tugging would begin.

At this point in the conversation, I felt like I was listening to a porn storyline even less likely than the ones on the porn DVDs I would win a few months later for coming in first place in Sircuit's Bear Chest Competition in Melbourne. I tried to wrap my head around the idea of getting a sponge shower by a beautiful naked stranger. What happened if you got aroused? If you grabbed him and started kissing him, did you have to pay extra? Were there condoms on hand just in case you wanted to take your steamy shower to the next level? Who applied for these jobs anyway?!

"At least you know he's clean," one of my lunch dates said, and he had a point. But while it certainly would have been better than getting a sponge bath from a cranky overworked nurse, I generally preferred to take a hands-on (my hands!) approach when it came to the washing of my nether regions.

From what I understood, the rest of the massage was pretty standard, except that the person rubbing you down wasn't wearing any clothing. I don't know what would have been most uncomfortable: being stretched out on a massage table in the nude, being straddled by a nude masseur or both at the same time.

The happy ending, by the way, was optional.

My lunch dates also told me about a show they had gone to the night before that, um, climaxed with two men actually having sex on a staircase. (Thank God they used condoms, which almost made it sound like live porn and a public service announcement rolled into one.) I'd once witnessed two guys fucking atop the bar in a dive in Tribeca, and that particular one in eight million stories in the naked city wasn't one I was in any rush to see again. I wasn't sure who had it worse in the voyeuristic scenario, the participants or the spectators. I knew some people liked to watch, but I'd never been one of them.

That was probably why I'd never gotten into porn, and ended up giving away most of my porn-prize booty (except for two DVDs, just in case I acquired a taste for it at some point). I didn't even like to catch myself in the act. It was the reason why I declined an offer to get rich quick by doing porn shortly after I moved to New York City, the reason why I turned down that guy in Cordoba, Argentina, who was willing to pay me for the privilege of sucking (then touching, then simply seeing, when I kept declining) a black dick, and one of the reasons why I never had sex in front of mirrors. There was a mirrored closet next to my bed in Buenos Aires, and I always had to position myself so that I didn't catch any accidental glimpses. If a videotape had ever surfaced of me in flagrante delicto, I would have gone into hiding for ten years. No joke.

Months after the X-rated brunch, at the encouragement of my Thai friend Tong, I decided to put my inhibitions aside. I checked them at the door and took a front-row seat to watch the onstage talent at Hot Male parading around and baring everything God gave them, which, in some cases, was considerable. (No, it's not necessarily true what they say about *Asian* men.) It actually hadn't taken much arm-pulling when Tong decided that it was time for me to lose my virginity — again. When I told him that I'd already given it up, having seen a male revue in Pattaya the previous summer, he laughed and said, "Not like this one."

From the moment we walked onto Soi Twilight, ground zero for gay sex shows in the Patpong red-light district, I had a feeling he was going to be right. Sex was in the air, and the stench wasn't all that appealing. It's one thing for sex-club personnel to try to entice you inside from a distance, but the ones here were practically mauling us as we wandered down the strip, looking for a show worth checking out.

We settled on Hot Male, where, for the price of one 250 baht drink ($8), you got to watch guys in white briefs with numbers attached sell themselves onstage (one wearing brown cowboy boots, a tuxedo-shirt collar without the shirt and briefs with the bedazzled word *sex* embroidered at the top, was working so hard to get my bid, I thought he'd jump offstage onto my crotch); near-naked showboys rolling around on the floor, covered in soap; and yet more of them strutting about with their junk hanging out. If you've seen twelve condom-covered penises dangling in front of you, you've pretty much seen them all, but I'll never listen to Robbie Williams's "Supreme" the same way again.

For the main event, two naked guys got onstage and gave us a tutorial on how to practice safe sex while swinging from bars, dangling sideways, hanging upside down and running around a stage. I was astonished by their stamina, their acrobatics and the fact that they were actually doing *it*. They were taking sex to brand-new heights — literally!

Looking at the bored expression on the face of the "top" and listening to the shrieks of the "bottom," not sure if he was expressing actual ecstasy or if it was just part of the act, I did the unthinkable: I started to laugh. Not just a giggle, but a loud guffaw from the depths of my belly. It was uncontrollable. Tong joined me. Thankfully, the crowd was too mesmerized by what was happening onstage to notice — or care.

I can't say that I was bored, but I wasn't turned on either. Some of the guys in the show were extremely handsome, and every time one of them winked or smiled at me from the stage, I winked and smiled right back. But there was something missing. They couldn't even get a rise out of me when a few of the showboys standing in the doorway to the bathroom patted my ass and tried to grab my crotch as I made my way downstairs to the loo. I didn't look back in lust or in anger.

As I watched some of the men in the audience purchase dates for the evening (for 100 baht, or roughly $3, they would sit down beside you and enjoy a drink — your treat, of course), I realized what was missing from sex as a spectator sport, this love for sale: the chase. I live for a good challenge, a feeling of accomplishment, the thrill of pursuit or being pursued. When you walk into a room full of hot males, all for sale, knowing that no one will turn you down if the price is right, there's simply nothing — or no one — to aspire to. Hot males at Hot Male were a dime a dozen, but for me, not even worth that much.

"Congratulations, Bangkok!" I said to the city as we exited and beelined to DJ Station, where the thrills were more PG-13. "You've accomplished the impossible. You've made sex totally unsexy."

I'm a Sex Shooter

Ah, life's little mysteries, the ones that might keep you up at night or drive you to distraction during the day. When I looked at the world, there were always certain unexplained phenomena that I zeroed in on, wondering, Why did anyone think of *that*? Like, who invented smoking? Who came up with checkers? Whose bright idea was chess? Who devised the ritual of watching sports (which might very well be one of the most pointless pursuits known to man, after smoking)? And what genius thought it would actually be cool to get women to use their vaginas as receptacles and dispensers for found objects?

That's entertainment?

Not for me, or so I'd always figured (not realizing how right I was). But my life abroad was about trying new things, and one Friday night in December, I did something I'd promised myself I'd never do. After a total of sixteen months based in Bangkok (ten of them consecutive), and less than two weeks before returning to Melbourne, at the request of an American girlfriend who was visiting Bangkok from Berlin, where she'd relocated from New York City eight months earlier, I took the final plunge. It was the one I'd been avoiding since I first heard about it from a female German tourist I was hanging out with on my fourth night in Bangkok the previous year: I agreed to go to a "Ping-Pong" show.

We had no idea which one to go to, so we were forced to depend on the kindness of a stranger — a man wearing a wig that looked like a turtle shell posing as hair who approached us as we were about to cross Surawong Road into red-light central — to lead us to the best one. If the place he guided us to was the top of the line among Ping-Pong shows, things must have been pretty grim at the bottom. As soon as I took one glimpse at the drab decor, I wished we'd stayed at Hot Male, where several cute showboys had been making eyes at me. But you only live once (or twice, if you're a James Bond fan who believes what Nancy Sinatra sang). Right?

And I really couldn't say I'd lived until I'd had the pleasure of paying 400 baht (about $13) to sit in a dark, nearly empty bar while an amazingly well preserved fifty-three-year-old woman (the proprietor — or madam — whose grown son was pouring drinks behind the bar) hit on me (Didn't the words "I'm gay" mean anything anymore?) and a procession of bored-looking women disrobed onstage.

The one with the most, um, skills — the apparent veteran of the bunch, she looked like she should have been reading bedtime stories to her grandchildren somewhere — did a stunt where she pulled a string with razor blades attached to it from her vagina, using one razor blade to engage in an arts and crafts project that she then presented to my friend and me, hoping for a drink in return. Note to sex-trade employees: If you have to beg customers for drinks and tips, you just haven't earned it yet, baby.

Another attached a Coke bottle filled with water and then one filled with Coke to her vagina, occasionally positioning her body so that the liquid trickled inside of her. I was terrified that she was going to pour the remaining contents of those bottles onto us.

The least enthusiastic showgirl of the bunch spent her entire time onstage just swaying to the beat like she didn't have a care or a spectator in the world, apparently too shy to remove the bikini top and bottom she was wearing. Did Maroon 5 know what these women were doing to its hit song? "One More Night" sounded a lot better with Adam Levine's abs providing visual accompaniment.

"What the hell is this?" I asked my friend as we watched the badly choreographed proceedings. In a city where hot females outnumbered hot males by a significant margin (not because there weren't plenty of attractive men, but because Thai women, in general, were so ridiculously genetically blessed), I couldn't believe that the owners of this particular Ping-Pong joint couldn't find one woman who could hold a candle (which, thankfully, wasn't one of the props) to any of the guys we'd just seen at Hot Male.

It had been my second Hot Male experience, and I still hadn't gotten used to a show that involved several groups of two having nonsimulated sex onstage. This time a few of them even took the act into the crowd for a little bit of audience participation. God must not have been listening to my prayer because one twosome stopped right in front of us so that the "bottom" could rest his head on my lap while the "top" stroked my chest. "How do they keep it in when they're walking around like that?" my friend asked as they returned to the stage. I didn't have a clue, and as much as I wanted to be a Bangkok host with all the answers, finding out that one wasn't on my to-do list.

I was equally at a loss to explain the vagina Olympics, too. Just as my friend and I declared that we'd had enough and were preparing to exit, the moment we didn't realize we'd been waiting for arrived. One of the women started to emit Ping-Pong serves from her vagina, while a customer seated in a chair in front of the stage tried to hit the balls with a Ping-Pong paddle.

Ping-pong. Ping-pong. Ping-pong.

"Please don't let one of them hit me," I prayed to God, who, this time, answered. I'd always hated Ping-Pong (speaking of things nobody ever should have thought to invent), but one good thing had come of watching this round of it: I knew if I ever got the urge to play with balls after midnight, I'd be sure where *not* to go.

Once we were back in the balmy Bangkok night air, I wondered why I'd had such a strong negative reaction to the female revue. It wasn't as if Hot Male was a bastion of respectability, but although I didn't necessarily approve of what they were doing onstage there, I can't say I didn't kind of enjoy watching them do it. Was I reacting out of a sexual distaste for female nudity — or women in general? Maybe I was holding women to a different standard of conduct than men. Or perhaps it was that shows featuring female private parts simply weren't created for gay men.

The latter certainly might have been the case, but I'd never had a problem with female nudity. Despite my sexual preference, I'd always been in awe of the beauty of the female form, and some of my best experiences with nudity had involved women. There was Marisa Tomei in *The Wrestler.* And there was the time in college when some of my friends and I drove from Gainesville to Miami to celebrate the twenty-first birthday of the second-youngest in our group. (I had nearly two months to go, so I used my brother Jeff's driver's license as my fake ID.) His dad took us all out for dinner and a lap dance. At the strip club, I fell for a naked Stacey Q look-alike who in turn almost fell into my lap.

"I think we've confirmed tonight that no one here is gay," the birthday boy announced at the end of our adventure with naked women. I wasn't sure if that was aimed at me or if it was just an innocent observation in a not-so-innocent setting. Whichever one it was, my enthusiasm while watching all of those naked women flaunt what God gave them in front of me had been no act.

But in Bangkok's red-light district, nudity wasn't sexy, and neither was sex. Hot Male and the Ping-Pong show were representative of one of my biggest problems with the Thai sex trade, an unfortunate dynamic that flowed over into the general population. When the emphasis was always on sex, especially in such a brutally forthright way, it began to lose its appeal to me. A surplus of sex created a deficit of desire.

A colleague once told me a story about how a country superstar she had interviewed told her he quit smoking by spending an entire weekend sucking on one cancer stick after the other. By Sunday evening, he never wanted to puff another one again. I guess the experiment could have gone one of two ways: the way it went, or it could have intensified his addiction. It might have been the same way with sex in Bangkok. The more some people got, the more they wanted, but because it was so often being shoved in front of my face there, my sex drive had never been lower.

Perhaps it was also the influence of growing up in the relatively prudish United States. Even in my wildest moments, I'd always been a closet Goody Two-shoes, and living in a city where I could walk down a crowded street in the broad daylight and have spa workers proposition me and guys try to sell me gay and straight porn, where I could go into a spa for what I assumed would be an innocent hourlong massage and end up being molested by a middle-aged woman, brought out my inner angel.

If she and I had been on a date, that would have been one thing. I wasn't above using a massage to get my way with someone. But there wouldn't have been any money exchange, no undercurrent of violence and pain, all key components of the entertainment at Hot Male and Ping-Pong shows as well as the professional Thai massage. For me, the latter, already such a rough experience, was much less rejuvenating with the threat — yes, *threat* — of sex hanging over it.

I once went out with someone who'd spent a year and half living in Bangkok, and he was celibate the entire time. "How is that even possible?" I asked him. By the time I left Bangkok, I got it completely.

I can't say the same thing about the Ping-Pong show. As extreme as the onstage action in Hot Male might have been, I understood its entertainment value. It was a joyous celebration of sex and sexuality that, in a sense, made fun of them both. Meanwhile, the Ping-Pong show was a bizarre onanistic display that no one — neither the performers nor the audience — seemed to enjoy. Not only were those women treating their private parts like toys, but they were using them as torture chambers, especially during the bit with the razor blades. It bordered on sadomasochism, which might have been one of my least favorite things to watch.

And on a purely aesthetic level, the Ping-Pong show was just such an eyesore. It was dark, drab and joyless, like a windowless one-star hotel room. The women weren't smiling, and neither were any of the six customers (including us). Naked women and their vaginas deserved so much better.

Come On, Baby, Make It Hurt So Good?

Never again.

That's what I promised myself the last time, after that Thai massage that went too far.

Never. Again.

But this wasn't just any night. After one week on Koh Samui, Nicholle, my best friend from high school and college, and her sister Noelle were in Bangkok for a fourteen-hour layover before flying home to the United States. I hadn't seen Nicholle since we celebrated our fortieth birthdays — which were two days apart — two and a half years earlier in Buenos Aires. And I hadn't laid eyes on Noelle live and in the flesh in more than twenty years.

We'd have to make their one night in Bangkok count, and few things scream "Bangkok!" like drinks at Lebua's rooftop Sky Bar, where scenes from *The Hangover Part II* were filmed, and an hour of body therapy in one of the myriad massage parlors dotting Silom Road. If nothing else, a massage would be the perfect intermission between dinner at Noodle and more drinks at DJ Station.

So inside we went. Noelle headed upstairs for her traditional Thai massage, and Nicholle and I settled into side-by-side recliners and waited for our foot-reflexology sessions to begin. I warned my therapist about the ugly bunion on my left foot (as if he wouldn't have noticed it) and begged him to be gentle. He nodded, but I wasn't sure if he'd understood a word I'd said.

After a short soak and rubdown in warm water — which would have been fine by me had it lasted the entire hour — I realized that he hadn't. He tore into my feet with wild abandon and gusto. I wasn't sure if he was trying to pleasure me or punish me. No part of my foot, bunion included, was safe from his aggressive rubbing, kneading, pulling and cracking. I wanted to scream out in pain. I looked around me. All the other reflexology customers were going through the same thing, but nobody else seemed to mind what felt to me a little bit like torture. I glanced over at Nicholle, hoping for some commiseration. She was fast asleep!

I resolved to toughen up and deal with it. There was a tall cute guy two recliners down. If he happened to glance over at me, I didn't want him to see me flinching and grimacing. Why did the gain from Thai massages have to come with so much pain? Oh, well. Some like it hot, and some like it rough. I'd just have to pretend that I was among the latter.

Come on, make it hurt so good!

Forty-five minutes later, it was over. And I had to admit, I did feel a lot better than I had when I walked in. I suppose that was the goal, but wasn't the journey supposed to be half the fun? For Nicholle, it was. Having her feet torn into had been so soothing, she said, that she had immediately dozed off. Noelle, who by now had come downstairs from her torture session, was elated, ready to tackle the long flight back to the U.S. The more pain, she insisted, the better.

I didn't know about that, but I had to admit that my hour of agony had left me feeling relaxed and rejuvenated, which was the happiest ending 250 baht could buy.

And the Horses Wonder Who You Are

Sex and sin city couldn't get more decadent than this.

Well, sure it could, but if you were a gay man and you didn't feel like dancing, you could indulge in Bangkok's debauchery without leaving the posh comfort of your five-star hotel room — or with a quick elevator trip down to those spotless bathrooms in the lobby. All you had to do was leave your inhibitions in the taxi that dropped you off at the entrance, and let the fun and games begin!

Oh, and you'd need your iPhone and a profile on Grindr, that boy-meets-boy app that revolutionized — though some might say ruined — the international gay dating scene and was putting even more bang and cock in Bangkok. If you were looking for fast love, it was the next best thing to just walking around with your junk hanging out.

Ready, set, *score*!

One night, months before I finally checked it out for myself, I learned a little more about the power of Grindr and the insatiable male sex drive when I went out for drinks with my twenty-two-year-old friend Tong. He told me some of the funniest, most horrifying stories I'd ever heard. Subject: what he did while he was on the clock at Anantara Bangkok Sathorn, where I'd officially been living for six weeks at the time. The term "guest relations" would never again have quite the same meaning for me.

So what was all in a day's work at the front-desk?

Checking in guests, checking out guests, *checking out* guests, luring guests into the bathroom for clandestine on-the-clock trysts. Think *Hotel* and *Fantasy Island* crossed with *Queer as Folk*. I would have included *The Love Boat,* but although water was optional, really, what did love have to do with it?

Thanks to Grindr, there was rarely a dull day on the job for Tong. Just whistle while you work? That was so old-school. He had a much better way to make his shifts fly by — which, come to think of it, easily could have involved whistling, humming a merry tune, snow white (Tong's preferred shade of guy) and perhaps even a dwarf or two.

He was almost always logged on to Grindr, as he was even while he was telling me his stories. When he was checking in guests, it was with his attention divided between the job at hand and a hand job, which he would likely score on his next bathroom break, courtesy of the iPhone perched conveniently by the keyboard. It was his backup gaydar, telling him who was close and ready to play.

Some of the men were hotel guests who'd checked in solo, with friends, with lovers (both male and female) or with wives. Some of them deepened their voices and put on their best hetero act, but Grindr pushed them out of the proverbial closet and into the public bathroom in the lobby, the one by the second-tower elevators that didn't have a dispenser filled with paper towels to clean up with after messy physiological reactions, like sudden sneezing fits or profuse sweating. The hot-air-blast machine only worked wonders with hands. The rest of their bodies would have to wait until the lift took them up, up and away, back to the privacy of the ablution chambers in their sleeping quarters.

Minutes after sending another new guest off to his rented temporary domain, Tong would glance down at Grindr to see who was around. Hot guy alert! "7 Seven meters away." He'd start typing.

Hi. How's it going?
Pretty good. Didn't you just check me in?
Yes, that was me.
I had no idea you were gay.
I didn't know that you were either.
Meet me in the bathroom in 15?
I'll be there!

Although I supposed he was only honoring the ultimate goal of his job, which was to make guests happy, I still couldn't believe what I was hearing. Sometimes he had this exchange of benefits several times a day, the record being, he told me, five in one shift. Apparently, he wasn't the only worker fooling around on the job. Everyone did it at all of the hotels in Bangkok (and in an increasingly app-obsessed age, probably in countless cities worldwide), Tong said, and not just gay employees with Grindr accounts. The female employees, all so beautiful and elegant when greeting guests, often went out to dinner with the guests before getting more intimate with them behind closed doors — though most likely not the ones on the bathroom stalls. As sex and the city goes, it might have been more Carrie Bradshaw than Samantha Jones, but the endgame was the same: optimal employee-guest relations.

As Tong was showing me head and cock shots of his Grindr scores, he told me stories of lust among the cannibals of Soi 4 in Silom's gay district, amid the big neon glitter of night-market stalls offering knockoff fashions, bootleg DVDs and souvenir trinkets, mobile food vendors serving up pungent Thai meals and freshly grilled insects, lusty go-go boys trying to entice patrons into their dens of iniquity, the occasional armless and legless man using his torso as human wheels, and cockroaches and rats scurrying across the sidewalk, seemingly drunk on the stale perfume of Bangkok's oppressive nighttime humidity.

In one of his tall tales, Tong was perched on the flaming-red terrace of Telephone Bar, across the Soi 4 walkway from our barstools in Balance, watching boys go by in real life and ogling them on Grindr, too.

Hot boy "2 meters away." Their eyes met on Grindr, then on Soi 4. Incoming message: *Meet me in the bathroom now.* It was hardly true romance, but this was Bangkok, not Paris in the springtime.

While this simultaneous browsing of two meat markets — one live, the other virtual — kind of made my head spin, I couldn't claim total innocence when it came to toying with beautiful strangers. My friends in Buenos Aires spent many a Saturday night laughing in disbelief as I worked the dance floor at Ambar la Fox, tossing one kissing partner aside for another, rinsing and repeating. I once had a play date with a twenty-one-year-old Argentine named Guido who couldn't believe he was out with me after having watched me sandwich him between two other conquests months earlier.

No, I was no angel. My friend Dave used to say that anyone in my path after a few drinks in any New York City watering hole became a human prop. I might have been the king of the short attention span, a queen who had seen, and possibly done, just about everything, but I had yet to disrobe on the job or enter a workplace bathroom for any purpose other than its intended use.

I doubted I ever would, but then, the possibility of getting caught had never given me much of a thrill. I might have been in the minority around Bangkok, though. Little did I know what was going on in the middle of the day fourteen stories down from where I went to sleep at night. Apparently, the bathroom next to the business center on the second floor could see as much action at 2 p.m. on a Monday afternoon as DJ Station on a Saturday night. And there was no 200 baht cover charge (two drinks included)!

At the time, I was a Manhunt vet but still a Grindr virgin and wouldn't start Grindr-ing until the following year during my ten-month second stint in Bangkok, so I knew I wouldn't be meeting up with any of my fellow residents unless it was purely by chance. And despite a hottie sighting or two in the gym, I hadn't spotted anyone worth making a special trip to the loo for. Still, perhaps I shouldn't have been so quick to send away that cute hotel employee who had delivered a case of bottled water to my suite a couple of weeks earlier during Bangkok's flood of the century, the worst deluge to hit Thailand in fifty years, when a mad citywide dash for emergency supplies had made it nearly impossible to buy purified water at the supermarket or any of the city's countless 7-11 convenience stores. But who was I kidding? I was much too shy to ever go there. I'd be picking up my next stranger with a Jack and Coke, not a mobile device, in one hand and a lame Rihanna remix pounding in my ear.

And if I ended up doing the walk of shame through the lobby the next morning, I'd have to remember to hold my head higher. Everyone watching me most likely had walked in my scuffed John Varvatos boots — sometimes more than once a shift!

Don't Stand So Close to Me

I always had this thing about strangers. I liked to keep them at more than arm's length. I'd never been much of a hand-holder, and I always hated kissing people on the cheek after just meeting them in Argentina. Why would I have wanted random strangers regularly invading my personal space?

Occasionally, I went a little extreme, and perhaps a tad bonkers, with my aversion to the nearness of strangers. If I was walking down the street and I felt someone walking too closely behind me, I'd sometimes stop and let them pass, just to avoid having some anonymous street-walker literally breathing down my neck.

In my mad pursuit of minimal physical contact with people I didn't know, I could maneuver my way through a crowded bar or club without once rubbing shoulders, or elbows, or anything, with anyone on either side of me. If only others possessed the same aversion to being touchy-feely in public spaces. Hands off the butt *and* the crotch, please!

My fight for personal space was never quite as lost as it was Friday and Saturday nights at DJ Station, possibly the most overpopulated place in Bangkok. For all of their emphasis on good manners, Thais could be disarmingly pushy. Maybe in the capital, the crammed sidewalks and traffic-jammed streets made them more impatient both on foot and behind the wheel. After sixteen months in Bangkok, I couldn't recall one driver ever giving this frequent pedestrian the right of way.

They were even worse when they were walking behind me at DJ Station. They often followed, hand on my back, as if that would get me — and by extension, them — from point A to point B more quickly. (Come to think of it, the locals did the same thing at Glam in Buenos Aires, but not quite as aggressively as in DJ Station.) How rude, I'd think, as I turned around and shot them a death glare.

Don't touch me there!

The only thing I hated more than being pawed by strangers was having to make small talk with them at the same time. I had to endure both one Tuesday evening when I settled into seat 1E on Jetstar Airways flight 30 from Bangkok to Melbourne and found myself engaged in meaningless chatter with the person sitting way too close to me in 1D. As he yapped away, I couldn't quite place his accent. He sounded like a German who'd spent so much time living in Australia and traveling abroad that he now talked a little bit like Johnny Depp whenever he played "European" onscreen.

Before he ever spoke a word, though, he had already gotten on my wrong side — my right side — by taking up too much of the armrest and making himself so much at home that I worried he'd drape his leg over mine just to get more comfortable. Through the corner of my right eye, I could see him glancing over at me, too.

Please don't speak, I thought to myself, mentally repeating it as if by some miracle of osmosis, my request would travel from my brain into his ears. It didn't. Soon we were touching on all kinds of trivial topics, which included how Jetstar had added an extra aisle of seats to its new fleet, meaning less legroom in business class. We should have considered ourselves lucky: Unlike everyone behind us, we were able to extend our legs all the way forward in our first-row seats.

I didn't feel so lucky, but at least he never asked what I was doing in Bangkok, or why I was going to Melbourne, or any of those travel-related questions to which I usually responded by handing over my blog URL and saying, "Read all about it."

Thankfully, once airborne, we spent most of the nine-hour flight in silence. He was immersed in some Bill Murray movie (*Groundhog Day*? But why wasn't he laughing?) on his iPad 2, or whatever high-tech machine he was staring at; I was trying to get some sleep. Every so often, I'd feel his eyes on me. I'd roll mine, as if to say, "Don't you dare say a word."

When we arrived in Melbourne, I made a hasty exit without saying goodbye. I felt a little bad. I wasn't sure why some people, like the one sitting behind me who'd barely closed his mouth for the entire flight, felt the need to engage the person sitting next to them on flights. Maybe it was boredom, or a fear of flying. If the aircraft went down in flames, you'd at least know a little about the person dying by your side.

But if I felt bad after I exited the plane, I felt terrible when I saw the man with whom I'd been stuck for the previous nine hours walking toward Immigration with his carry-on in one hand and some kind of telescoping cane in the other. WTF! I had no idea. He was visually impaired? Didn't the same thing happen to Blanche on *The Golden Girls*? Actually, it did, twice: once with a blind man, another time with a millionaire in a wheelchair. Boy, were her powers of observation shot or what?

I wanted to go over to the guy with the cane and offer some assistance, or apologize for not being nicer throughout the flight, though my silent departure aside, I'd been perfectly polite every time he'd spoken to me. Testy as I could be in public spaces, unless you were poking me in the back at DJ Station, I generally griped on the inside.

As my former in-flight neighbor walked away while tapping the ground with his cane, I was thankful for the one upside to his visual impairment. At least he probably never even noticed me rolling my eyes at him.

Excuse Me If I Start to Play with Your Digital Display

One day I got the ping I'd been waiting nearly two years for. It came via Skype, from someone I'll refer to simply as G — and not because he was even remotely gangsta.

G is for *gorgeous:* tall (at least half a head over me, and I'm six-foot-one), dark, handsome and possibly the best kisser I met in my entire four and a half years living in Buenos Aires. We never went out on an actual date, never made awkward conversation after bumping into each other on Avenida Santa Fe or after waking up together on a Saturday or Sunday morning. I don't think I ever even saw him in the light of day.

The only face-to-face conversations we ever had were well past midnight as music thumped in the background, at Rheo, at Human, at Ambar la Fox. There was an obvious physical attraction, but the fact that he never tried to do anything about it, never busted any of those cheesy *porteño* pickup moves I'd come to loathe during my stint in Argentina, made him even more appealing.

The only time we made actual physical contact was one Saturday night at Ambar when we gave in to passion — sort of — and spent fifteen minutes making out by the coat check. Just when our body heat was rolling toward a full boil, he pulled way, reluctantly, and said he had to leave. I tried to get him to stay. He invited me to go with him. I considered it for a full thirty seconds before politely declining. I had to look after a friend who'd had a bit too much to drink and had issued me a warning earlier: "If I suddenly lose consciousness, don't panic. I'll probably only be out for about fifteen minutes." I suggested that it might be time for us to leave, but my friend insisted that was just a worst-case scenario, an unlikely possibility.

I wish I'd pushed harder because then I would have been long gone by the time G showed up, and he wouldn't have become my sort-of-one-who-got-away. A bit melodramatic, yes, but as he walked out the door, I knew my window of opportunity was closing for good. In Buenos Aires, guys didn't take rejection well, even if it was less rejection than "Maybe some other time." I had boys throw mini-tantrums and storm off just because I said "I'd like to see you again, but I'll be leaving alone tonight."

G skipped the theatrics, but a few days later when I sent him a Facebook message asking him out on an actual date, he didn't even reply. At least he didn't delete me or, worse, block me on Facebook, I told myself by way of consolation. It wouldn't have been the first time.

Thus began six months of silence. Then one day, G surprised me with an invitation to add him as a contact on Skype, the form of online instant communication I used least at the time, possibly due to my aversion to video-call requests. Who needed to see me lounging around at home in track pants and a *Mr. Perfect* T-shirt? I would have become a Skype devotee for life, though, if it meant that G and I might pick up where we'd left off that Saturday night at Ambar. There was, however, one huge logistical problem. By then, I was living in Australia. In the end, it didn't matter because, like so many people who added me on Skype, on Facebook, on MSN Messenger, G never actually said anything to me.

Until that fateful day when the ping arrived that put a little bit of kick into what had started out as a fairly mundane afternoon.

Hola.

My heart jumped and then fell. Hard. The lack of an exclamation point after the greeting wasn't a good sign. Argentines never forgot the exclamation point if they were really into you. And if he was in Buenos Aires, it was past 2 a.m. No guy in BA ever called, texted or pinged after midnight on a weeknight unless he had one thing in mind.

Or maybe he was going to tell me that he was in Bangkok. Another unlikely scenario, but at least we were communicating again. I took the bait.

Hola! I didn't forget the exclamation point!

Como va — Wait, no question mark? He must have been really drunk, really horny or both — *Todavía vivís en argentina?*

Damn, I thought. He's definitely not in Bangkok. I had to break the news to him that I hadn't been living in Buenos

Aires for almost exactly one year. Obviously, he hadn't been paying attention to my Facebook status updates or reading my blog.

Ok

I smelled the unmistakable whiff of his losing interest coming from my laptop screen. Trying to keep the conversation going, I told him that I'd spent the last year living in Australia and Thailand.

Ah hace mucho

Well, a year isn't really that long, but whatever. I wondered when he was going to get to the point.

Estoy medio caliente. Te va hacernos unas paja?

There, he said it! He wanted us to have hot and sweaty Skype sex. Now, I'd done a lot of things in the name of lust — text sex, outdoor sex, kitchen sex, shower sex, rooftop sex, three-way sex, normal two-way bedroom sex — but one thing I'd never done (besides 35,000-feet-above, up-in-the-air sex) was take it off in front of a computer screen. And even if I were to accept his invitation, would he be there in the morning — *his* morning — or at least by the six o'clock news?

Once again, I politely declined. This time, my excuse was that it was shortly after noon in Bangkok and I had a lot of work to do. Like my previous excuse, it was actually true. Had he been in Bangkok, though, I would have dismissed those deadlines for a few hours. But the problem with computer sex, aside from the fact that it would be a little weird, was that I found it kind of pointless, too. An afterglow cuddler and unashamed of it, I sometimes endured the rest of sex just to get to that part, the *good* part.

What worked for Michael Fassbender in the movie *Shame* just wasn't for me. "I've got to remember to try that sometime," I said to myself, staring at the big screen at Kino Cinemas in Melbourne as he got off while staring at the small screen on his laptop. I knew full well that I'd never do anything of the sort.

If regular body-to-body sex when two people lived in the same city seldom led to anything long-lasting, what hope did two people jerking off in front of their computers on different continents have? I was flattered that G had thought of me — especially after more than a year of ignoring me — but if I was never going to hear from him again, I didn't want him to remember me *that* way, pants down in front of a computer screen.

Now there was a look I knew wouldn't look good on anyone, except maybe Michael Fassbender in *Shame*.

We All Feel Better in the Dark

There's nothing like walking through rooms without a view, as multiple hands poke, prod and grope you, to make you appreciate living in the light.

Hello, sunshine. It's nice to see you again. I think I'll stay a while.

One year and two months after my first arrival in Bangkok, I experienced a gay rite of passage that most queens plunge into before they've unpacked their stash of condoms. I went to Babylon: not the Biblical contemporary of Sodom and Gomorrah, but Bangkok's premiere — and possibly only — totally gay luxury hotel. Though I wasn't expecting to go out in a blaze of fire and brimstone, I had a feeling that He wouldn't have approved of some of the stuff that was going down there either. Not that I actually *saw* any of it.

I went with Tong, who for months had been regaling me with tales of his escapades within Babylon's darkened halls. Thanks to my slightly prudish streak and the superfluousness of a hotel with on-site "dark rooms" (the kind where condoms and lube, not film and stainless-steel reels, are the tricks of the trade) in a city where you can get a happy ending from pretty much any massage therapist for less than $10, I resisted any urge I may have had to do more than live vicariously through his tall tales of tall men in the dark.

Then one Thursday night a taxi driver changed my mind.

"Silom Soi 2," I announced when I got into the cab.

"Oh, you're going to DJ Station," the driver said. Then he started singing a strange made-up song with "DJ Station" as its only lyrics. "Have you been to Babylon?" he asked around what I assumed must have been the bridge. "Sathorn Soi 1." New song, new lyric.

I wasn't sure if it was an invitation or just some friendly information from a taxi driver to someone he figured was just another horny gay tourist looking for a thrill during a few days in Bangkok, but my curiosity was piqued. Now I knew where the famous Babylon was located — right along my thrice-a-week running route en route to Lumpini Park. And I'd thought the only action around *there* was on the jogging track and in the bushes off to the side of it, where the freaks went when they came out at night!

It's not every day when a straight guy (and I presumed that's what the driver was) gives two thumbs up and a song and dance to a capital city's gay mecca. If it was good enough for him . . . A few days later, I told Tong that I was ready to enter Babylon's unchartered (by me) territory.

My first impression after our arrival was that it wasn't at all what I had expected, which was a seedy-looking facade with a tacky-posh interior design, sort of like those icky love motels in Buenos Aires. It was actually a four-star(ish) boutique hotel with a pool, several bars, a gym and a restaurant that served excellent Thai food.

Oh, and there was also a maze of dark rooms where hotel guests and visitors (100 baht for those younger than thirty,

260 for everyone older, which seemed to be most of the Western clientele that Friday evening) could retire for "fun," to use that annoying euphemism for sex that was being overused even by grown men who should have known better. I wasn't interested in any of that, but I stripped down to my swimming trunks anyway because I wasn't about to walk around wearing nothing but a towel.

"So what exactly do you like about this place?" I asked Sonny, Tong's friend who'd come to Babylon with us, as we sat by the pool. He seemed bored, like he was only tolerating the experience. But as it turned out, he was quite the Babylon regular.

"I just like to come and touch a little bit."

Oh, so that's what else they were calling it! I liked it better than "fun, and it sounded a lot safer than what I imagined was going on behind those closed cabin doors. Just as I was mentally approving, Sonny excused himself to go get touched.

After dinner, Tong took me on a guided tour of the grounds. I couldn't believe the things I saw — or, rather, couldn't see — as we walked through the darkened maze leading past the cabin doors in the play areas. I laughed nervously as hands grabbed my ass and crotch, swatting them away at first before balling up my towel and using it as a protective shield in front of me. I would have been flattered by all the attention, but it had nothing to do with me. The owners of those untamed paws couldn't even see what I looked like.

Sonny suggested that I was such a hot commodity at Babylon because I was exotic (as in black), but weren't we all the same color in the dark?

I'd never been so relieved to be back in the light — until I ran into the French guy who'd been chatting up Tong and me only minutes earlier. Finally, it all made sense. It didn't mean I'd ever revisit Babylon, but at least I got it. As we stood face to face, my eyes darting from the patchy sprouts of fuzz growing on Frenchie's head to his furry shoulders and his protruding belly, I realized that he'd left his most flattering lighting on the other side. Like the Eiffel Tower when it lights up at night, some things just look better in the dark.

V. XXXs and OOOs

On My Side of the Bed

Despite its positive airbrushing properties, for as long as I could remember, I'd been afraid of the dark. That might have been why I was always such a hopeless insomniac. I closed my eyes at my own risk.

Still, even on the deepest sleepless night, I normally had better things to do at 5 a.m. than reach over and fondle the person lying next to me. But Andrew and I had been dating sporadically for nearly two months and frankly, I was feeling pretty horny. Though we hadn't done anything more than make out, for the first time we were sleeping together without any clothes on, an arrangement that I'd instigated.

I'm not sure what I was expecting when I reached over and grabbed his cock, but it certainly wasn't what I got.

"Please, let me sleep."

Deflated for what wasn't the first and what wouldn't be the final time during our strange courtship, I rolled over and stared at the glass partition separating the bed from the bath and beyond, replaying our short romance in my mind.

Our first encounter had been some fifteen months earlier, a few hours after my first arrival in Bangkok. I was browsing through the local profiles on Manhunt, and I spotted Andrew's. I was pulled in by something about him, though nothing in particular. It's not like he was the cutest guy I'd come across during my search, though he certainly was one of the blondest, and nothing he wrote in his profile made a particularly strong impression.

   I think part of it was that he looked like the type I never seemed to get — his face was the classically cute, perfectly symmetrical sort that rarely directed its gaze in my direction — and I was feeling brave. I seldom approached anyone, online or off, preferring to let them come to me (while setting the tone of the courtship, why *shouldn't* I let him make every move?), but I decided to test my confidence and sent him a "wink."

   I wasn't really expecting a return "wink," but a few minutes later, there it was. After the perfunctory introductory messages, I asked him out. I invited him to meet me that Saturday night at my hotel, Lebua at State Tower, the one featured in those rooftop scenes in *The Hangover Part II*, for drinks, and he accepted. I felt like I'd won the lottery *and* gotten the guy.

   Alas, my celebratory mood was premature. A mere fifteen minutes before our appointed meeting time, Andrew sent me a message telling me that something had come up and he wouldn't be able to make it. He didn't explain why, and I didn't press. "I'll be here until Monday, so let me know if you want to meet up," I wrote back, certain I wouldn't hear from him.

   I was mildly disappointed (no sweet kisses tonight!), slightly relieved (no awkward banter either!) and totally unsurprised. I'd always had a sixth sense for these things, and mine had been nagging me all afternoon, saying the date wouldn't happen. Hey, I thought, at least he didn't just not show up. More than a year later, when I mentioned the incident, of which he had zero recollection, he said it sounded like him and described himself as a classic Manhunt "time-waster." If only I'd taken that sign and run away with it. Of course, then I'd only have half a story.

Andrew also had no memory of our second interaction, that one face to face. He said it was probably because he was too drunk at the time, making it sound like a common occurrence. Another sign?

He's British, I figured, that's what they do. They kiss and don't tell because half of the time, they can't remember. Much to my disappointment, there was no kissing that night either — at least, not with him.

We met at DJ Station by the second-floor bar, where I was holding court with cute passersby in my usual spot. He was standing next to a woman, who struck up a conversation with me and introduced her cute friend. "Jeremy, this is Andrew." I knew it was the same guy who'd blown me off several months earlier, but his face didn't betray even a hint of recognition. I'm not sure why, but his friend seemed intent on our getting together. So did Andrew — some other time. He asked me for my email address, which struck me as unusual, since when I went to ask the bartender for a pen and paper, he stopped me, pulled out his phone and saved it there. I had no idea why he didn't ask for my phone number, too, but I was pretty certain I wasn't going to hear from him anyway.

It was just as well that I didn't. I was still picking at the battle scars from my breakup with Shane a little more than a month earlier, occasionally causing them to ooze blood. I couldn't say they were completely healed the following August when I found Andrew again on Manhunt, but by then I was resigned to living with the blemishes. Life must go on.

Though I'd been on only a handful of dates since my postmortem lunch with Shane in February and hadn't had sex in three months (since my second date with Jorge, an Argentine world traveler who'd found me on Manhunt in April), I was ready to spend more time in the dating pool by August, if only to wade in the shallow water. In a replay of the scenario from a year earlier, I sent Andrew a "wink." Same script, same cast.

This time, he didn't cancel our date, which was on Friday, August 24, 2012. It was easy to remember the exact day because that afternoon, Alison Moyet tweeted me right after I tweeted her a link to the blog post I'd written celebrating the thirtieth anniversary of the release of Yaz's *Upstairs at Eric's* album.

Thank you Jeremy. Really. xxx.

If Andrew didn't have me at hello, he got me when he understood what a big deal it was to receive a tweet from Alison Moyet, which was even more impressive when you considered that he was born in 1983, the year after *Upstairs at Eric's* came out. He increased his standing with me when he took me to Bar 23, an indie-rock pub in Sukhumvit where the DJ played Happy Mondays, Stones Roses and Elastica, among other retro Class of '90s acts, and Andrew revealed that R.E.M. was his favorite band. Mine, too!

"I figured you'd like it here," he said when I told him how much I loved the shabby-chic dive filled with English-speaking expats. A fellow pop-culture nut with excellent taste in music, and he got me: Could it possibly get any better than that? Well, it might have had he done more than walk me outside and hug me goodbye after I announced I was leaving.

For the next few weeks, I wasn't sure if our platonic text exchanges with occasional sexual innuendo thrown in (like my subtle suggestion that my bathtub was big enough for two) would lead to friendship or more. I was having so much trouble reading Andrew. He was clearly interested, but in what I wasn't sure. I knew he wasn't going to make the first move, so on our second date, emboldened by Johnnie Walker and Coke on a Friday night, I grabbed him on my couch and kissed him for the first time. When he kissed me back, passionately, I was sure we'd turned a corner.

At 2 a.m., after two hours of making out punctuated by occasional commentary about whatever was on TV, he announced that he had to leave. He'd been up since 5 a.m. and he had to wake up early the next morning for a mattress delivery between 7 and 10 at his apartment in Ari, near the Victory Monument, thirty minutes by taxi from where I lived in Sathorn.

"If I spend the night, I know I won't get any sleep at all," he explained apologetically. I wasn't sure if he was just trying to make a graceful exit until he suggested we hang out the following evening. That night, I was the one who didn't get any sleep because I spent the next several hours tossing and turning in bed, giddy with glee over our great date, anticipating our next one.

It was the perfect setup for Saturday love, but I should have known better than to have harbored such great expectations. When I texted him the next afternoon to see what he wanted to do that evening, I began to wonder if maybe we'd been on two different dates the night before. Had our Saturday-night plans been only a tentative, worst-case scenario in case Andrew didn't have anything better to do? Apparently, he did: a big birthday dinner that I wasn't invited to.

Maybe we can meet up later?

I knew a blow-off when I saw one, and when I still hadn't received another message from him at 10 p.m., I texted him to find out if we were meeting up.

A few minutes later, incoming message: *Still at dinner. Not sure what we're doing later. I'll text you at midnight to see what you're up to.*

If I wasn't positive I was being blown off then, after a few more similarly noncommittal text messages, I was convinced of it. Feeling defeated and disappointed, I took to Facebook, hoping to find a friend online with whom I could commiserate. That's when I noticed an unread email in the "Other" folder that had been sent two days earlier. No way!

It couldn't have been . . .

Hey Jez. I've been thinking about you a bit lately and thought I'd send you an email. I just wanted to see how you're doing and say I miss you I guess. I hope this is okay. Shane xxx ooo.

Once again, I spent the night tossing and turning in bed, dwelling on Andrew, then on Shane. Was this yet another sign? If I'd thought about it before, Shane would have been the long-lost person I most wanted to hear from and the one I least expected to contact me. The email had arrived early on Thursday morning, 4:29 Bangkok time, which was three hours behind Australia, but the timing of my reading of it (around midnight on Saturday) was impeccable — and curious, too. Was the universe trying to tell me to refocus my romantic energy on Shane?

It was the most unexpected and pleasant surprise — in a sense, he'd saved my life, or at least my sanity, that night — but I wasn't sure what to make of what he'd written. Did he want me back? I kept re-reading the "I miss you I guess" part, saying it in different ways to convey different meanings. Eventually, the romantic in me triumphed. I composed my response — his sentiments exactly ("I miss you, too"), with a heart-shaped cherry on top — and wondered, Was it time to let Andrew go and allow Shane back in?

As I waited for a response, I convinced myself that the early morning timing of Shane's email must have meant he was still drunk from the night before and therefore not thinking clearly. I tried to reshift the focus back on Andrew. After a few days of ambivalence and a declined invitation to meet me after he finished work (something about already having plans with his sister and then a dumb joke about how he was "an in-demand guy"), I told him that the next move would have to be his. He apologized for being "a bit rubbish," whatever that meant, but offered no further encouragement. Two days of radio silence followed, so I did what any self-respecting romantic intent on moving on would do: I deleted him on Facebook. End of story in twenty-first-century dating!

It would be another week before I'd hear from Andrew, in the form of a Facebook email. He said he knew I must be angry since I'd unfriended him (I wondered when he'd first realized it and how), and he wanted to explain himself. There had been someone else, a man he'd known for a couple of years with whom he'd been flirting for several months, since his final days with his ex. ("Stuff happened," he wrote. "Not much," he was sure to add, presumably to convince me that their interactions had been as chaste as ours up to that point.) The other guy was hot and cold and had been sending Andrew the same mixed signals that Andrew then forwarded to me. He told me it wouldn't have felt right starting something up with someone new until he was sure things with the indecisive one wouldn't lead anywhere, implying that they hadn't. He was sorry for handling it badly.

You're a nice guy, and I wish you the best in life in

general. Infamous last words. I wondered why he even bothered.

I would have asked the next night when I ran into him in DJ Station, but the vodka he'd been downing with his friends all evening had turned him into a different person, one who was openly flirtatious and affectionate. He apologized over and over for his negligence — and his inebriated state — throwing in several passionate kisses. "If I were you, I would have deleted me on Facebook, too," he admitted during one of our breaks for air. It was the best thirty minutes we'd ever spend together, mostly because it was the only time he did all the work. I wondered if he'd remember in the morning.

As it turned out, he did, though only bits and pieces. He insisted that the sentiments he'd expressed were real, even if he didn't quite remember the specifics of them. Our next few dates, all suggested by him, were sweet, though not exactly the kind to move the relationship in any definite direction. One night he invited me out for drinks with his sister. That didn't shock me nearly as much as when he held my hand in front of her, with neither fanfare nor any hint of discomfort.

If only closeted Shane could have been so open with me when we had been in public. We'd been talking on Facebook for several weeks (in one of his emails he mentioned that he'd finally come out to his entire family, and everyone, especially his dad, had taken it well), but with Andrew doing and saying all the right things, and Shane holding back just enough for me to question both his true intentions and what I continued to see in him, some of my affection for my ex was beginning to recede into the background. Sometime around 1 a.m., as I rode home alone in a taxi, and later when I crawled into bed, I wondered if tonight would be the night that the ghost of Shane would finally stop haunting me.

Alone Again, Naturally

Three mornings after Andrew touched me in front of his little sister, I was lying in bed, halfway between hungover and still tipsy from a Sunday night out with my friend Sam. Dangerously in lust, I sent Andrew a series of incriminating, amorous text messages. *I like you.... No, I'm crazy about you,* I typed into my cheap mobile phone and pulled the covers over my head, waiting for him to freak out or to never hear from him again.

Much to my surprise and delight, neither happened. Within moments, he responded: He liked me, too! *In fact,* he'd written, *I actually had an idea. It might be too soon to ask you. Maybe I'll leave you in suspense until I gather enough courage.*

I encouraged him to go for it.

Tee hee, erm. Well, I'm going to Krabi the weekend after next for a few days, alone, king size bed...

My mind was boggled. I'd known about his Krabi trip, and I can't say I hadn't considered the highly unlikely possibility that he might ask me to join him, but I figured he'd be far more likely to extend an invitation to lunch or dinner with him and his visiting mom than to lock in four nights in a king-size bed with someone he hadn't even had sex with yet. It wouldn't exactly have been a first for me, but then I was the one who'd asked Lucas to accompany *me* to Colonia five and a half years earlier, and that was only a one-night sleepover for a visa run. This would be a proper holiday, and we'd be traveling together by plane, not ferry, which made it a much bigger deal. Maybe I was misunderstanding Andrew.

Is that an invitation?
Yes, it is an invitation.... There's only one condition.
What would that be?
You have to add me on Facebook.

As I honored his request, a nagging voice inside my head, one I'd been trying to ignore for weeks, once again interrupted my glee to tell me that this wouldn't end well. How could it? Could there possibly be a happy ending with an admitted time-waster, especially one with alcohol-induced forgetfulness who popped Xanax pills like they were Tic Tacs? It wasn't so much the time-waster comment, or the fact that he didn't remember either of our first encounters the previous year, or the fact that he was obsessed with his smartphone, or even the fact that we hadn't had sex and I wasn't sure if he wanted to.

There was a blankness in Andrew's blue eyes that I couldn't help but notice every time I looked into them. It's the reason why, whenever I kissed him, I'd always cut it short so I could open my eyes and see if his were staring at me, blankly. They never were, but I still couldn't shake my mistrust. The following Sunday morning when he told me about the massive row he'd had with his mother a week earlier, one that resulted in her flying back to the U.K. two weeks sooner than scheduled (which would have made an invitation to dine with them less likely than I'd thought), I rationalized that I'd had my own turbulence with my mom. Who was I to judge?

But I couldn't get past those blank blue eyes, the fear that there were no feelings behind them, which is why I consulted with several friends to get their take on my travel plan (they all approved), though in my heart I secretly knew that this getaway for two would never happen. I figured he'd rescind his invitation and I'd be secretly relieved. Could a loner like me even handle a weekend in tiny close quarters with a hot-and-cold guy who didn't seem to know what he wanted — or if he wanted anything at all?

At times he seemed like a composite of my two most significant expat-era boyfriends, Lucas and Shane, a combination platter of their worst qualities. As with HIV-positive Lucas, there was a dearth of sex, which often made me wonder if Andrew was hiding something just as big. At least Lucas had been relatively consistent, unlike Shane and Andrew, who was constantly messing with the thermostat — freeze, thaw, freeze, thaw, freeze, thaw — even more so than Shane ever did, and more often than not setting it on just above ice.

I think part of why he oscillated so wildly may have been his own lack of connection to Bangkok, despite having lived there for three years. I always got the sense that Andrew didn't really know what he was doing in Bangkok, and his general dissatisfaction with his life bred intermittent periods of malaise during which he retreated emotionally, usually with the assistance of Xanax. He wasn't sure what he wanted in life, or romance, or even for dinner. A few days before our departure to Krabi, he sent me a text message telling me that he'd be embracing vegetarianism while we were away, or trying to.

Um, why? I responded, bracing myself for what I was sure would be an annoying answer.

When in Rome...

Do as the Romans do? I completed the thought in my head. Like learn the language? Although over the course of three years living in Bangkok, he hadn't bothered to learn Thai, every year during the annual ten-day Vegetarian Festival, he went above and beyond the call of culinary duty by giving up chicken, read meat, duck and any other formerly living and breathing edible.

I figured that was one way to feel connected to a culture if you didn't have any interest in communicating with the natives in their own tongue. Another concession to the Thai way: Whenever he entered my apartment, he took off his shoes, even after I told him he didn't have to. I, for one, had no interest in feigning assimilation. Although I'd spent more than a year in Bangkok off and on, I still considered myself to be only passing through.

Andrew wasn't sure where he'd ultimately end up, but for the time being, Bangkok was his home by default. He had his full-time marketing job at Canon, which he appeared to hate, and a social circle that seemed to include family members (his father had been living in Thailand for years, and his sister was in the process of relocating in Bangkok) and fellow U.K. expats.

I'd been wondering why I was having so much trouble connecting with people in Bangkok, and Andrew offered me some clarity. It was a city overpopulated with tourists and locals who were looking for sex and not much more, and fellow expats who were wandering as aimlessly as I was. They were all searching for something to make them feel connected to a place that, thrilling as it might have been, rarely seemed to feel quite like home to outsiders. I'd never identified more with the outsider complex than I did in Bangkok, and my sort of misery loved Andrew's sometime company.

After more than six months in Bangkok (which was just enough time to make you start to wonder what the hell you were still doing there), our slowly budding relationship was like a small lifeline in a place where I had begun to feel like the walking dead, more alone than I'd ever been in Melbourne or Buenos Aires. That must have been why I put up with so much of Andrew's crap and why I hadn't made a single close friend in a city full of people (mostly expats) who spoke my language. My expat associates in BA were much more settled into their lives abroad, unlike most of the expats I encountered in Bangkok, who all reeked of transience.

It was hard to connect with people who felt so rootless, too, always wondering if today was the day, if this was the week, the month, the moment, that the winds of change would blow them away. The ones who had managed to make themselves at home in Bangkok wore their Thai friends like badges of honor in public, sort of the way their Thai friends clung to their token *farangs*. They all had their perfect accessories, so they didn't have any use for me.

I heard somewhere that nobody who spent more than thirty days in Thailand wanted to leave. But the smart ones didn't settle too long in Bangkok and usually ended up far north or south of the capital. Bangkok was a good place to lose oneself while in a holding pattern as I was — writing, freelancing and trying to figure out the next professional move — but like the rarified air over a landing strip, it wasn't necessarily a place where one wanted to linger too long. Andrew characterized his relationship with Bangkok as being one of intense love-hate. They gave each other mixed signals. They were hot and cold. It didn't escape me that this was how he seemed to conduct his romantic relationships, too. It was certainly how he was with me.

Hot plus cold equals lukewarm, which leaves a lackluster sensation. But it burned red-hot on Tuesday evening when Andrew finally sent me the text message I'd been expecting for days. Something had shifted in him during our date the previous Saturday night — the one when I fondled him. The next morning, I felt a chill; a cold front had moved in. When I kissed him, he kissed me back, but there was something tentative in his kiss, like he was trying not to get too into it.

And then there was Shane. He was back in my life, albeit only by Facebook email. Between "I miss yous," he claimed he hadn't contacted me hoping to get back together but rather because he hated it when exes pretended the other didn't exist. He also revealed three emails in that he was seeing someone and things were, in his words, "kinda serious, I guess," leaving me to wonder why he picked that particular time to decide that exes should be in each other's lives.

He confused me further when he called me three times at 1 a.m. (4 a.m. Australian time) the night that I was naked in bed with Andrew, who I still hadn't told him about. Groggy and feeling guilty because my incoming calls had woken up Andrew, too, I got out of bed, went to the living room and turned off the phone during the second series of rings without reading the number on the display.

When I didn't answer, Shane sent me a message on Facebook, which I didn't read until the following morning after I realized that he had been the mysterious caller. In it, he apologized for the phone calls (he'd been drunk, naturally) and for complicating my life by re-entering it, and twice again he told me he missed me. He really, really missed me. It had been one week since he'd last emailed me, reluctantly telling me about his new boyfriend (*I wasn't sure how to tell you,* he'd written), and I'd yet to respond. *When I didn't hear back from you, I was worried,* he said in the latest email, which was surprisingly coherent, considering his inebriated state when he wrote it. *It's not like you to take so long to respond.* I had to chuckle at the irony.

The timing of his three phone calls, however, wasn't so amusing. Why now? And why on the night when I was naked in bed with Andrew, hours before he rebuffed my amorous advances? Was Shane's once-again uncanny timing the latest in a string of filed-away signs that Andrew and I were not meant to be? I was still trying to decide what to do with the coincidence that both Shane and Andrew had two-year-old nephews named Mason. I didn't have much mental space left. Where was I supposed to process *this*?

Everyone drunk dials an ex at some point, Andrew replied several hours after I texted him late Sunday afternoon, dutifully telling him about Shane's calls, hoping to elicit even a twinge of jealousy. It was the first of three days of texts that he'd take hours to respond to without offering any excuses. In the past, if he was even thirty minutes late in responding, he'd always offer a reason why, possibly because he knew that I knew how attached he was to his phone.

Perhaps I was giving my insecurity and neuroses too much power, but I'd always had a particular skill for reading people and situations, especially when there was a negative spin. I started having flashbacks of Kevin, the guy who dumped me while I was on holiday in Rio ten years earlier.

The day before my departure, he'd suddenly iced over, too. I knew what was coming with Andrew. I spent days walking around with knots in my stomach, waiting for it.

On Tuesday, three nights before takeoff, the moment I'd been expecting with dread arrived in the form of two text messages in which he finally said everything I knew he'd wanted to say since I touched him *there* on Saturday night.

Maybe I'm overthinking things, as is my habit... the first one began.

"Here it comes," I whispered, bracing myself.

He suggested that we "not rush into things," that we look at the holiday as a "chance to unwind, get to know each other better, see what develops." My heart sank a little.

"I'm just worried that you might be looking at this as being some big step forward," he said over the phone a few minutes later. I had texted him back, demanding that he call me. "I don't want you to be disappointed if it's not." For someone who claimed to be thinking about my feelings, his words were showing a complete disregard for them.

He wanted to act like we were just two friends going away together ("Because we *are* friends, I hope"), though if I remembered correctly (and I knew that I did), his text-message invitation had mentioned something about a "king-size bed," which is not exactly what you use to entice a "friend" to go on holiday with you unless it's understood that benefits would be involved.

When I asked if he wanted out (because he clearly did), he

insisted that he didn't. I asked about the one who'd gotten between us before. Was he still in the picture? Andrew assured me he was long gone and wouldn't be making a comeback. During our back-and-forth, he made a few clumsy attempts to shift the blame for the recent chill to me, citing my too-breezy text messages (*Morning. How are you?* I'd had the nerve to write to him on Monday) and my "inappropriate" early morning groping. I found his prudish streak to be thoroughly disingenuous and hypocritical, especially considering that we'd met on Manhunt, and he was parading around Grindr shirtless.

Eventually, he gave up his losing fight and apologized. A few minutes after we hung up, he reinforced his apology with a contrite text message. He shouldn't have said anything (his official assessment, not mine, though I agreed).

The next morning, he sent another SMS apologizing for "sounding like a complete dick" the night before. I accepted his latest apology, though I was already thinking of ways to bow out gracefully. Later on, he invited me to have after-work drinks that evening, and as I got ready to meet him, I felt like I was preparing for an audition. Both of us would be trying out for the role of potential travel partner, more than a week after we'd been cast in the parts. I wondered what had possessed him to invite me on this trip in the first place. And why, pray tell, had I accepted? I barely knew the guy, and I was beginning to wonder if I wanted to.

As I sat across the table from Andrew at the pub while he

fiddled with his smartphone, I shifted in my seat so that I was facing the window, not him, and pretended to be too busy looking at some interesting scene unfolding outside to care that he was being unbelievably rude. When he bothered to turn his attention to me, he was glum and cranky. I thought that maybe his foul mood was due to the Xanax he'd popped a few hours earlier. Then he told me about the fainting spells and bouts of temporary blindness his sister had been having for weeks. Could this have been the reason for his ill humor? But his voice hadn't betrayed even a hint of worry; he could have been talking about the friend of a friend of a friend of someone he used to know. Was it the Xanax?

"Has she been to the doctor? She needs to be very careful about this. My sister was having similar symptoms before she was diagnosed with a brain tumor last year."

"Why are you telling me that? Fuck! I don't need to hear that right now! That's not what I want to hear!"

I couldn't believe he'd gone from barely conscious to boiling rage in the space of a few sentences. I'd never seen him angry before, and I wasn't sure how to respond. In the end, I didn't. I held up my hands and conceded defeat. "I'm sorry I said anything."

I knew that the audition wasn't going well for either one of us. I started having flash-forwards of myself sweating in a bungalow in Krabi without AC, swatting away mosquitoes and trying to hatch an escape plan as he sat on the king-size bed fuming over something I'd said — and tap-tap-tapping on that damn smartphone. Would I escape to my own hotel room (AC included)? The next flight back to Bangkok? After declining his invitation to have another round of beers, I knew it was time to make my preemptive strike. When he finally put down the phone, I felt my mouth moving involuntarily, and words were coming out.

"I don't think it would be a good idea for me to go with you to Krabi."

"I was starting to think the same thing. You don't seem like you want to go with me anymore. But what changed? Was it our conversation last night?"

"Partly, but I already had my doubts. Ever since Saturday night, you've been acting strangely, and tonight you're just being nasty. It's almost like you're trying to make me not want to go with you."

"I'm not accepting the blame today," he said, his voice rising. "This is *your* fault." He then proceeded to list all the offenses I'd committed in the last hour, from my lack of repartee (yes, I'd set my own bar pretty high) right down to my body language. How rude of me to sit sideways in my chair, with my body facing the window instead of him!

As he continued shooting barbs, I stood up and, without a word, without a glance back, walked out of the pub, leaving Andrew sitting alone at the table. Within an hour, he'd unfriended *and* blocked me on Facebook!

Meanwhile, I had a big decision to make: Should I stay in Bangkok that weekend, or should I go to Krabi? It was a no-brainer that I answered as quickly and decisively as I'd left Andrew sitting alone in that pub: Why should I give up a trip to Krabi just because I knew it would be a terrible idea to go there with *him*? I banished all thoughts of canceling or postponing the trip and booked my double accommodations for one. Two mornings later, I was sitting on the one-hour-and-twenty-minute AirAsia flight from Bangkok to Krabi in the rear of the aircraft with my former would-be travel partner a dozen or so rows in front of me, probably tapping on his smartphone. I was so relieved that I'd never have to sit across from that again.

When we landed in Krabi, I was feeling brave and independent, but by the time I got into the taxi, my confidence was wavering. I'd seen Andrew buying a bus ticket near the airport exit, and I could feel his attention on me as I ordered a taxi. I tried to play it cool, but I knew I was talking too loudly. "How much is a taxi to Ao Nong beach?" I asked, trying to ignore the guy in my peripheral line of vision. Mission accomplished, but I was starting to dread the possibility of running into Andrew unprepared over the next few days.

I wasn't sure if I'd chosen wisely by going after all, but a few minutes into the cab ride, I knew that I had. Driving routes from airports to hotels are typically flat, drab affairs, but cruising along, gazing up at the high-rise rock formations off to the side, I felt like I was traveling through a postcard paradise. How had it taken me so long to get here?

Dear Mr. Helligar & Partner, began the welcome letter in my suite at Vogue Resort & Spa. I wondered if the proprietors had been spying on me over the course of the last few days and now were taunting me for my hasty change of plans. Then a text message arrived from Sam. He was in Krabi. He wanted to surprise me, so at the last minute he and his houseguest booked a twelve-hour bus ride from Bangkok to Krabi. About a half hour after I received his text, they were in my lobby.

Normally, surprise visitors weren't my thing, but it was nice to be distracted from my own thoughts for a while. I was happy for the company and the glimpse they gave me over lunch of what might have been. Watching Sam struggle to communicate with his Thai friend in English, observing his growing frustration as the person he'd been spending the past week with paid more attention to his smartphone than anything or anyone else, I knew that despite that awkward *Dear Mr. Helligar & Partner* greeting underneath the Vogue letterhead, I was lucky to be a solo act in Krabi.

As much as I was looking forward to hanging out with Sam outside of Bangkok, I was more eagerly anticipating the time I'd be spending alone. For a recovering introvert like me, quality time with a friend was always best when it ended with a quick goodbye, and me alone, again, naturally.

Oh, No! It's You Again!

Hey Jez Balls. Thank you so much for last night. It was amazing. xoxo I think I had the best sleep ever. It was so good to see you again. xoxo I should probably stress that I'm really in no position to pick up exactly where we left off. The last month has been horrible with the break-up and everything and I don't know where I am at the moment or what I'm doing. I really want to see you again though. xoxo I just don't want to give you the wrong idea. I hope this is okay. Seeing you has made me so much happier. xoxo Shane

As morning-after text messages go, it left much to be desired — and not just because it was syntactically challenged. It's not like Shane could ever be bothered to use commas to organize his thoughts.

But I preferred the text message he'd sent the morning after we first met two years and three months earlier. Since then, however, I'd learned not to expect the best from Shane. And though it was by far the longest, it wouldn't be the only perplexing text message he'd send me over the course of the next month and a half, culminating with the one that arrived two days before Valentine's Day that finally broke my cycle of stupidity.

The week of Valentine's Day was not exactly a good one for love. The implosion of my rekindled romance with Shane (or whatever one would call that awful pattern we'd fallen back into) was sandwiched between a string of dating disasters. First, there was Saturday night with Marty, a twenty-three-year-old university student from Estonia with a penchant for traveling across the globe to meet strangers he'd found online. I wasn't aware of this particular proclivity when I agreed to meet up with him at Father's Office, a "speakeasy" bar and restaurant across from the State Library of Victoria in Melbourne's CBD. Had I known, I would have saved myself the $3.50 train fare from South Yarra to 249 Little Lonsdale Street.

I couldn't say I was into Marty at all. His upper torso was too concave, his teeth too far apart, and what was with his travel bug? He'd just returned from a two-week trip to California, a holiday he said he'd planned in order to connect with a guy in San Francisco whom he'd "met" online. Alas, they had a huge fight a few days before Marty's departure date and broke up before they even got together. I wondered which one dodged the biggest bullet.

I considered bolting when he excused himself to go to the bathroom an hour into the date, but I couldn't bring myself to be so insensitive. So I stuck around and waited. And waited. And waited. After ten minutes, he hadn't returned. I feared he'd had the same idea that I did and had beaten me out of there. But with my clear view of the exit, there was no way he could have pulled it off unseen.

Just when I was about to go to the bathroom to investigate, Marty reappeared, holding his mobile phone up to his ear with one hand, pointing to it with the other and making that "Important call!" face. Then he disappeared onto the terrace. After another ten minutes, I decided it was time for me to make my dramatic exit. I chugged the rest of my raspberry cider, stood up and walked out, hoping that he had a clear view of my departure. After my adventures with Andrew and his texting during dates, I wasn't in the mood. I never again heard from Marty, who had spent weeks trying to score a face-to-face date with me after spotting me on Grindr. I guess that was one effective way to get rid of an unwanted guy.

If only it had been so easy to extricate myself from Shane. I'd texted him on December 16 to wish him a happy twenty-fourth birthday and texted him again a week and a half later to let him know that I'd be back in Melbourne on January 4. When he invited me to dinner, I accepted, wondering if his boyfriend would be joining us. But after a week of flip-flopping, during the nine-hour Jetstar flight from Bangkok to Melbourne, I decided that I shouldn't have any contact with Shane after I arrived. My resolve was short-lived: When I received a text message from him, almost as if on cue, just as I was entering the hotel room where I would be spending my first night — *Welcome back to Melbourne! Are we still on for dinner tonight?* — how could I not respond?

Sure. Why not? I decided to play it cool since he wasn't. Obviously, he was eager to see me, or his timing wouldn't have been so perfect. When he offered to come to my hotel, I figured that the boyfriend must have been out of the picture, too, or he would have suggested a public meeting place. I was hopeful, but not too much, lest I be disappointed when he showed up and just wanted to be friends.

Shane arrived at my hotel fifteen minutes before our appointed 8 p.m. meeting time (apologizing for being a bit early as he announced himself by text), and when I went downstairs to meet him, rather than waiting in the lobby or just outside the entrance, he was pacing back and forth on the sidewalk, well out of immediate view, just as he had been the night of our first official date. His hair was longer and tied back in a high ponytail, he had a full beard, and he'd gained a noticeable amount of weight (thirteen kilos, he'd later reveal).

It felt like the hottest day of the century (forty-plus Celsius), so although he'd taken the tram nine hundred meters from Barkly Street, where he was now living, he was sweating like he'd just run a mini-marathon. He looked so different than he had at Burger Edge nearly a year earlier, but when we greeted each other with a hug, it felt like we'd last seen each other only yesterday.

It was just like old times, which that night was a bonus, but would prove to be a bad sign since old times weren't really as wonderful as I'd been remembering them. We bought a six-pack of Pure Blonde beer and another of Jim Beam and Coke, and two footlong Subway sandwiches, and returned to the hotel to watch the bootleg DVD of *This Is 40* that I'd picked up on Silom Road in Bangkok. As Shane figured out how to work the DVD player, I mentally replayed a near-identical scenario from nearly two years earlier at my South Yarra rental. Shane was so good at figuring out where wires and plugs went and what those mystery keys on remote controls did.

While we were catching up, first eating across from each other at the coffee table, then sitting side by side on the bed, he told me that he and the guy he'd been seeing had broken up a month earlier. They'd been living together (in separate bedrooms, he was sure to point out, and with five other people), and he had moved out because the roommates were the ex's friends first. I was relieved, though I should have asked more questions: How had they met? Why did they break up? Were they still in contact? Why did they live with five other people?

Instead I stuck my head in the sand and let my heart lead. When the DVD player gave out halfway through the movie, I handed him the remote control so that he could channel surf. Just like old times. That meant we were paying more attention to each other than to the TV, darting from topic to topic, inching closer and closer. Soon we were kissing and undressing each other, caressing, nibbling, sucking — tender foreplay followed by sex for the first time since we'd showered together on the morning before my first departure to Bangkok a year and a half earlier.

His ears were as sensitive as ever, his body below the

neck softer but still ticklish. He remembered all the erogenous zones he had taken so many months to finally pinpoint (tip of my tongue, nipples, tip of my tongue, nipples), though as before, he lacked the knack for properly stimulating them. Why couldn't he just keep it right there, keep it right there? I felt like Tantalus being continually teased with the fruit of life (Shane's tongue wrestling with mine, or gently gliding over my nipple) only to have it pulled away too soon. My ex still had the attention span of an average twentysomething: He hadn't fully grasped the idea that the journey is more important than the destination.

But so what if the trip was not quite a rocket ride? It was familiar and comfortable, mind-blowing not for our technique but for our still-powerful emotional connection. We spent the entire night wrapped around each other. I even may have slept a little. By the time we went for round three as the sun came up, I was falling in love again.

An hour after his departure the following morning, the unsettling text message arrived. I was used to Shane's hot-and-cold, but to go from one extreme to the other in the space of a few sentences was a new record for him. Most of my friends told me I should run, not walk, away after I told them what he'd written. It was pretty presumptuous of him to assume that I wanted us to pick up "exactly" where we'd left off, as if that was a place worth going back to. I couldn't understand why he didn't just leave it at "It was so good to see you again." Why overthink things so much? I texted him back telling him we were on the same page, and it was the truth. But why did he have to ruin our perfect night together with so many morning-after clichés, especially since I hadn't said or done anything to suggest that I was expecting an instant reunion?

I understood that things weren't great with Shane. Both of the internships he'd been hoping for after graduation had fallen through, and he'd taken a part-time job in a menswear boutique on Chapel Street in addition to the restaurant where he'd been working since before we met. He'd been living with friends since breaking up with his ex, and he still wasn't sure if he was going to continue with school or focus on finding a full-time job in his field. It's not as if the world was brimming with job opportunities for recent design graduates. Shane's life was pretty much one big question mark. I got that; I could relate. I just didn't understand why he had to praise me and push me away in the space of one email.

I should have insisted that we talk about it in person, or at least in real time, the way I had with Andrew when he'd sent me a similarly deflating text a few months earlier, but I was too jetlagged to try to solve another puzzle. I decided I'd let Shane control the course of the things, as usual. That meant weekly text messages, a date where he showed up at my apartment when he got off work and fell asleep after sex and a shower, and a drunken Saturday night phone call the following weekend to remind me he was still alive and that he missed me. Two weeks later, he turned up again, well past midnight and drunk, after sending me a text message asking if I hated him, apologizing for being an "insensitive dick" and begging me to let him come over and kiss me and spoon me to sleep.

That night, which would end up being the third and final date, kicked off a week of apologetic behavior. What he was sorry for, I couldn't say. He was doing a lot of alluding, but as usual, no real communicating. And I was too afraid of what he might say — was his hot-and-cold behavior now due to lingering feelings for the ex? — to push him. What was he trying to tell me?

After the third date, I began making a greater effort to steer us toward the type of reconciliation that I wanted, which would have involved more than a late-night shag every few weeks. I had previously been riding shotgun, playing it cooler than ever in the passenger seat, responding to his texts with as few words as possible, never instigating communication, which I suspected might have led him to believe I hated him, hence the apology for being an "insensitive dick." After explaining to him that I was only trying to give him his space (to which he replied, "That doesn't mean I don't love . . . spending time with you"), I decided that it might not have been what he needed — or really wanted. It was time for me to take charge.

But the hotter I got, the cooler he became. He was receptive to my requests for his company, but I sensed a holding back, more of a polite enthusiasm than genuine ardor. When I extended a spontaneous last-minute invitation at 7 p.m. to join my friend Marcus and me for Wednesday night Bingo at the Greyhound Hotel, he said he was keen to go, but he wouldn't be finished making dinner, eating it, and reinventing the wheel, until well after 10. By 10:30, I was ready to go home and crawl into bed and he, apparently, was too tired to text more than five words at a time. I made a joke about black dildos to which he responded *LOL,* followed by *You're funny.* Good night.

On Friday when I asked If I could see him that weekend, he said maybe Sunday night if he wasn't too tired after spending the weekend at his family's beach house, but he ended up blowing me off completely and going out with his friends after getting back to Melbourne.

I almost called you drunk last night, he finally texted on Monday, shortly after noon.

So when am I going to see you? I resisted the urge to be snarky.

I work on Tuesday and Wednesday. I could come over after?

I'd love that. So how are you doing?

I'm okay. You're so much better to me than I deserve.

I had no idea what he meant by that, but it was a fitting setup for what he did the next night, something he'd never done before: He broke plans with me. At 10:30, he sent a text message saying that he wasn't feeling well and would probably be going straight home. *Can I come over tomorrow after work?*

Already have plans. Don't worry. Feel better. I wanted to be as breezy as possible.

Ok, thanks. x

I didn't understand his current obsession with xxxs and ooos. Had he always been such a slave to trite niceties?

Thirty minutes later, another text arrived: *Are you upset with me?*

I couldn't take the cryptic half-apologies any longer. Clearly he realized he was being an asshole, yet he kept on being one. I felt like we were reliving 2011. Aside from his being out of the closet and his now being as obsessively attentive to his iPhone as everyone else, he hadn't changed. He was now twenty-four and always attending birthday parties for friends turning twenty-five instead of twenty-one, but emotionally, he was still acting like a teen, still using booze as a communication crutch, still using *an* instead of *and*. He seemed more unattainable than ever, and I was tired of reaching for him.

After two and a half years, hadn't we evolved past late-at-night booty calls? Didn't I deserve more? Why was he still pulling me to him with one hand (the florid once-a-week text messages calling me "big beautiful man," telling me how much he missed me) and pushing me away with the other (the cold shoulder he'd turn to me the rest of the week, or whenever I instigated any kind of connection)?

I gave myself a night to think about it, and at 3:15 a.m. I came up with the perfect response, which I delivered three hours later, on the morning before Valentine's Day: *LOL, I'm not upset. Far from it, in fact. I've lost interest.*

At 6:45, I heard back from him: *What a difference a day makes. Fair enough. I understand where you're coming from. Jeremy, I'm really glad we were able to reconnect. All the best. x*

He never called me Jeremy, always "Jez Balls," even after we'd broken up, and I couldn't believe he'd finally used a comma. I had a flashback to our lunch a year earlier when he didn't take off his sunglasses. I felt like this was the text-message equivalent of his attitude that day. He was trying so hard to be the good sport who didn't really care that I no longer cared.

Only I did. But it was true that I wasn't upset. I still felt a powerful physical attraction and emotional connection to Shane, but I wondered if what I initially mistook for resurrected love had been more like lingering affection for him. I'd always care about Shane, but perhaps what had drawn me back to him romantically was the security and comfort of having him in my life again. Could we possibly have been in love by that point? If we had been, wouldn't we have tried harder to have an actual conversation rather than trade such complacent text messages and then leave it at that. Unlike the last time we'd broken up, I couldn't even be bothered to respond. I deleted his number from my phone so that sentimentality and temptation wouldn't sway me. Shane would have the final word.

I had no regrets. I'd done the right thing. I had to go backwards with Shane, remember why he and I hadn't worked in the first place, in order to stop idealizing the past and move forward. Now if only the past would stop coming back to mess with my present.

Ruined in a Day

The lack of resolution in most parts of my life — still no job, still no publisher or agent for my book (*this* book), still no end to the apartment debacle in Buenos Aires — made me particularly vulnerable and susceptible to the charms of returnee loves (Shane!) and lusts, like Clint.

My first encounter with Clint came one Saturday night during my first holiday in Melbourne, some two weeks before I met Shane, at the appropriately named Disgraceland. My friend Marcus had just gone to the bathroom, leaving me alone on the dance floor, but not for long. One moment, I was trying to catch the attention of a tall, handsome, blond guy while losing it near the stage with my broad-semaphores-as-dance-moves to the pumping remix of Stevie Nicks's "Edge of Seventeen." The next, our bodies were pressed together, bumping and grinding, simulating the motions I was hoping we'd be going through in private after closing time.

Alas, nothing else happened between Clint and me that evening. He vanished as suddenly as he'd entered my orbit, without leaving me so much as a kiss to remember him by. We wouldn't make it to first base until some six months later, after I had moved from Buenos Aires to Melbourne. After spotting me on the corner of Chapel Street and Toorak Road one balmy afternoon and then finding me later on Manhunt, he sent me a message requesting the pleasure of my company some enchanted evening, like that Saturday night.

I was reluctant to go there. Things were going pretty well between Shane and me, but I knew it wouldn't last for long. And Clint *had* called me "stunning," which was hyperbole at its most flattering. I was impressed by his gallery of Manhunt photos — though he seemed a little too comfortable baring it all online — so I agreed to meet up with him on Saturday. As usual, Shane had plans with his friends, so what harm was there?

It ended up being a fantastic date, just the sort that Shane and I would never go on. We began with drinks at Cookie, one of my favorite places in the CBD, then dinner at a Pan-Asian restaurant a few streets over, followed by drinks at two swanky bars — one rooftop, one underground — that I knew I'd never be able to find again.

It wasn't until we were at the second one that I finally let Clint kiss me. I'd been wondering what it would feel like all night, and when our lips finally came together, they were close to a perfect match. Ours was one of those effortless makeout sessions that easily could have gone on for hours. I didn't even care that we were in a straight bar, and everyone very well may have been staring at us. That was part of the thrill.

When he said he was dying to get me naked, I was tempted to oblige, but I declined his invitation to go back with him to his hotel. Shane had been text messaging me for about an hour to see if he could join me, and in the end, I blew off both guys — though, unfortunately for them, not in the way they would have liked me to. Enjoyable as the evening with Clint had been, all along I had known that he saw it as merely an appetizer for what, in his mind, would be the main course.

But he had it backwards: Our date up to that point had been an elaborately prepared and luxuriously consumed multicourse meal. I could have stepped away from the table perfectly sated. Had Clint expressed his continued craving with more subtlety and less desperation, dessert might have been his for the devouring, but his hokey come-ons — "I just want you in bed with me. I promise, we don't have to do anything" — all felt too Hookup 101. As for Shane, I wasn't interested in listening to his drunken declarations of love.

I didn't expect to hear from Clint two years later, two days after Shane had blown off our tentative Sunday-night date to get drunk with his friends, but he had excellent timing. At last Grindr (which was where Clint found me this time) was good for something, having given me a reason to suspend my brooding over Shane. Clint was in Melbourne for the night, staying at the Como, which was less than one kilometer from my apartment on Darling Street in South Yarra. I agreed to go over at 7 p.m. This time, I was determined to let him sample the sweets.

I had just gotten out of the shower and was drying off my body, anticipating the good times dead ahead, when it arrived — another one of those unwelcome text messages, this one from Clint.

Will you bring some lube over with you?

I didn't know which was worse, that he'd just assumed I'd have a stash of lube, that he was so certain that full-on intercourse was part of the plan, that he'd already assigned our sexual positions (me: top, him: bottom) or that he clearly only had sex on the brain. I told him that in addition to not having lube, I never fucked anyone I wasn't dating, but there were plenty of other things we could do. Was he OK with that?

It was a bit of spin control intended to get me out of doing something I simply didn't enjoy, whether I was dating someone or not. I'd spent most of my time with Shane wondering when he'd bring up intercourse, but to his credit, he only did twice, and both times he was drunk. Shane was so vocal, demonstrative and excitable in bed — I don't believe anyone ever made me feel like I was more skilled there. But I still always worried that he thought something was missing, and to me, the fact that he brought it up a second time was evidence that he did. It was the last time we had sex, when he came over drunk at 1 a.m. As he was sprawled on top me while I was lying facedown in bed, he asked the question I never wanted to hear.

"Do you have any condoms?"

I told him I didn't, and that was the truth. I was relieved when he dropped it, but I searched his face for any sign of disappointment. I didn't see one, and his screams of passion afterwards suggested that he was perfectly satisfied — for tonight. But was I missing something? As I usually did with Shane, I was second-guessing myself. I wondered if he'd remember in the morning asking for a condom. I knew that eventually we'd have to talk about our sex life — my fears, his desires, his expectations, whether he was a "top" or a "bottom" — and over the next few days, I rehearsed in my head the conversation that we might have the next time we saw each other. The one good thing about breaking up for the second time a week and a half later was that we'd never have to have that talk. It was just one more example of how a lack of communication poisoned our relationship, which was why I wanted to be more open with Clint, who responded as I'd expected him to.

Cool, he texted back. I knew there was more coming, and it took only a few minutes for it to arrive.

Do you mind if I go to the gym later. I got the point. If he wasn't going to get it from me, he was going to get it from someone else in the shower. I told him to go ahead to the gym and give me a call if he felt like getting together later. I knew I wouldn't hear from him, and he didn't disappoint.

I never thought I wouldn't hear from Nicholas, the guy I met at The Peel less than forty-eight hours after I'd cut Shane loose again. When I went there on Valentine's Day evening, I was hoping for a repeat of the night I'd met Shane there two and a half years earlier. I couldn't believe it when lightning struck twice in almost the same exact spot, on another Thursday night. First there was a beautiful girl, Victoria, who was visiting from London. She introduced me to her friend Nicholas, and we hit it off immediately. Unlike the night I met Shane through his then-girlfriend (unbeknownst to me at the time), there was no question about the nature of Nicholas's relationship with Victoria. He was clearly gay. As if to underscore that point, before long, we were making out in pretty much any spot both of our bodies would fit into — even in the stall of the unisex bathroom!

Predictably, we lost each other after about an hour. At 4 a.m., he sent me a text message. *It's Nicholas. You are very, very sexy.*

At 4:29, another: *Are you still at The Peel?*

I'd just left — with another guy. Of course, I didn't mention that part.

At 4:30, yet another: *I really want to see you again.*

I wouldn't get that text until the following morning when I woke up in bed with the other one, whose name immediately escaped me. It was 9:30. At 8:14, Nicholas had sent a photo of himself lying naked in bed, facedown. I flashed back to the email that Shane had sent me the morning after the night we met. I couldn't believe I was reliving that experience with someone else, right down to my not leaving The Peel with him, though this time the after-party was for two, not three.

The next afternoon, Nicholas and I began exchanging text messages. He asked if I was on Facebook, and added me as a friend. He said he thought he'd seen me leaving The Peel with some blond. I told him that we'd left to get food (a giant gyro for two from an after-hours eatery on Smith Street), but I left out the other details. I couldn't believe he was still interested. We decided to go out for dinner and drinks the following night. When he texted me later in the evening, just to see how I was doing, I thought I might have found the perfect rebound guy who could actually turn into something more. I didn't even mind that he was only a few months older than Shane.

I celebrated too soon. When I texted Nicholas on Saturday afternoon at 1 to make a firm plan for that evening, I expected to hear back from him almost immediately. By 5:30, he still hadn't responded. I decided I wouldn't play games. I was particularly vulnerable after my week with Marty, Clint and Shane. I really needed Nicholas to be different.

So are we on or off tonight? I never heard back from you.

About fifteen minutes later, he responded: *Some friends dropped by unexpectedly. I think I might have to take a rain check.*

Ouch.

How nice of you to tell me this so early. Don't worry about the rain check. I'll pass. Send. Delete — from my phone, from Facebook, from my life.

It was like two and a half years of Shane squished into thirty-six hours! I didn't know what had turned Friday's romantic fervor into Saturday's indifference, and it was none of my business. If things with Nicholas were going to begin so badly, I didn't even want to think about where they might have led. His blasé response several hours later — *Okay* — minus any attempt at an apology, and another Facebook friend request two days later (ignored, of course), told me I'd dodged a deadly bullet.

At least I knew I was learning from my past mistakes. I may not have been anywhere near the vicinity of happily ever after, but I was making progress.

All Apologies

November 22, 2013
 7:10 a.m.
 Hi Jeremy!
 I don't know if you remember me . . . (though I have a strange feeling that you do)
 I was reading old fb messages and I came across one of yours, about some post in your blog that talked about love songs and sad songs.
 I went to your blog and went back to 2009 and started checking those of the period we were dating . . . And I decided that I was going to write to you.
 We didn't break up in the best terms . . . And I think that an apology was necessary.
 I was . . . a child, in some way. I was terribly scared of taking things further. Don't ask me why, because I do not have that answer, or perhaps I do . . . I wasn't ready, not because of my feelings for you, but for what people would say — especially my family! I mean, I was dating a guy who was the same age as my mum! It would have definitely been weird for them.
 I've grown up now, changed in many ways (and haven't changed in others: I still like Harry Potter, Transformers and all those things). I even have a tattoo now (on my chest, and it hurt like hell!).
 I've been in a relationship for almost four years now . . .

Anyways, I'm missing the point. I wanted you to know about all that . . . I wanted you to know that I am sorry for the way I was with you. You did not deserve it.

Now that I've made my catharsis . . . I want to know about you! How are you, Jer?

Love,
Gejo

Holding Out for a Hero?

The chapter titles in this book were inspired by song titles and lyrics. I wanted to call the final one "How I Got Over," but the truth is, I still hadn't, not completely. One year after I'd last heard from Shane, I continued to think about him daily, though no longer all day long, usually only for a few moments at a time here and there when I passed someone on the street who reminded me of him. It happened enough with guys who didn't look anything like him for me to know I hadn't reached that elusive state of closure.

At least I didn't look back in sadness. When I thought about Shane for more than several scattered moments, I was less overwhelmed by longing and regret than by questions: Had he ever loved me? Had I ever loved him? Why hadn't he tried harder? Why hadn't I tried harder? Why was he still invading my thoughts? Was I still part of his daily mental routine?

What went wrong? That one was easy: We simply didn't work. I resisted the urge to assign all of the blame to our age difference. I had listened to the gentle admonishments of my friends ("What were you thinking? He was too young," they all said — or clearly wanted to), and while I was thankful for their concern, I rejected their age-old age argument. I knew it was more complicated than that. Relationships between people of the same age failed all the time. All of mine had.

People get so caught up in age (even while claiming that it's just a number) that they often forget that more than anything, our character, not our age, makes us who we are. Shane out of the closet at age twenty-four was practically identical to Shane in the closet from twenty-one to twenty-three, only hairier and heavier. He was still waffling, still uncommunicative, still bravely honest only when drunk dialing (or texting, or emailing), still apparently uninterested in what was going on in my life.

Maybe that was just his character, who he was and who he would be, regardless of his age. As much as I'd matured and evolved since I was in my early twenties, I was still essentially the same person at forty-four. A bad match in 1993 still would have been a bad match in 2013 because, as Luke Spencer on *General Hospital* once said, "People don't change. They just get older."

In the nine months after that final pre—Valentine's Day text message, I didn't hear anything from Shane, which was both a relief (as the Oscar Wilde—quoting sweatshirt that my mom bought for me as a kid read, I can resist everything except temptation) and a source of frustration. The previous year he'd let only seven months go by before finally reaching out to me; nine months of silence had passed this time. Was it really over for good?

Why did he relight my fire when I was in Bangkok and he in Melbourne, only to go even more hot and cold than usual the morning after our Melbourne reunion? I suspected it was because he was still fighting feelings for his other ex. On another morning after, the one following our final night together, he woke up from weird dreams. The one he recounted began something like this: "I was in my ex's family's home, but he wasn't there." I thought it was an inappropriate and brutal thing to say while in bed with me. It was another aha moment when I knew for sure that he had to go — again.

If he and *that* ex had been so tight, why had he contacted *this* one again while they were still together? Why not ride off into the sunset with his latest flame and leave me to my latest doomed romance? Why had I taken the bait? If he was sending me such ardent emails while living with someone else, who knew what sort of emails he might have been sending that former boyfriend after leaving my bed? Shane had, after all, sent me that very first amorous text message two years earlier while lying in bed with his girlfriend.

For all of my lingering questions regarding Shane, there was no question that I was going through a change. When it came to love, I was a different person in 2013 than I had been in 2010. I'd grown increasingly wary of romance, not that anyone was offering it. As Grindr had made sex more accessible and less meaningful, I'd become less interested in it, often going months without so much as kissing anyone. Had I met Shane then instead of three years earlier, you probably wouldn't be reading about him right now.

It wasn't just about Shane. Years of romantic

disappointment, online and off, in New York City and later in Buenos Aires, Melbourne, Bangkok and all of the places I visited in between, had taken an emotional toll, leading to recurrent celibacy. They'd turned me into even more of a suspicious person than I'd been before, convinced that all men were just out for sex. Grindr and PlanetRomeo and nights out on whatever town I happened to be in kept proving me right. The approaches may have varied, depending on the country they were made in, but the motivation was usually the same.

 Nobody seemed to be looking for anything more substantial than "fun" or "no strings attached." I installed barbed wire over the fortress around my heart, making it even more difficult to access than my bed. But nobody was climbing into either. I was becoming more of a loner, prematurely morphing into the near-recluse I never thought would emerge until I was well into my old age.

 By the Northern Hemisphere summer and autumn of 2013, when I spent a month apiece in Berlin, Rome and Tel Aviv, I'd folded up my penis and put it away. Even in Tel Aviv, the so-called gay capital of the Middle East, I wasn't interested in meeting the men who approached me on Grindr, most of whom asked the same one-word questions ("Looking?" "Fun?" "Sex?" Hung?"), like they couldn't even be bothered to type sentences, and I sampled the scene only a perfunctory handful of times. When I did, it was always the same shit, different men: *Show us your big black dick!* If I didn't grant them instant gratification, they moved on to the next one.

In the modern world that had changed so much in seven years, one where you could tweet your every thought to millions of people in 140 characters or less, go viral in hours with only a smartphone and a YouTube account, and get promoted from unknown to American Idol in less than six months, patience was no longer a necessary virtue. Nobody wanted to wait for love or work for a hookup, and they no longer had to. Grindr, the virtual sex club, had seen to that.

I didn't give up on love completely, though, and my experience with Shane didn't lead to my padding my deal-breaker list. I couldn't imagine ever again getting involved with anyone who wasn't completely out of the closet, like Shane when we first met (or Lucas, or Gejo), but I wasn't ruling out a future boyfriend who was half my age. I just wasn't buying the argument that twentysomethings were inherently worse for me than men in their forties. I'd dated enough of my contemporaries to know that they were not necessarily more mature or well adjusted. Being older certainly didn't mean you had your shit together. It's not like I lived happily ever after with any of the people my own age whom I dated before my late thirties. It's not like any of those relationships were easier — or better.

I loved how fearless younger men were, at least in the beginning, before the reality of commitment kicked in. They just dove right in, taking huge leaps of faith without overthinking everything. I hated that we rarely had the same points of pop-culture reference (for example, Gejo's *Transformers* obsession and Shane's love for the *Glee* version of "Don't Stop Believin'," which he heard before Journey's 1981 original, and which he still preferred afterward), but I would rather have committed to an enthusiastic twentysomething whose iPod was stocked with bad pop music than a middle-aged man whose romanticism was tempered by a long list of don'ts and who was terrified of losing control.

    Any therapist worth his wages in hourly fees might have told me that Shane's youth had been a double-edged sword, one that had pierced right through my heart's armor and was still twisting around, splattering blood all over my recovery. His youth had been part of what attracted me to him in the first place, and it was an even bigger part of what had kept me obsessing over him in our aftermath and what continued to make my knees buckle slightly whenever I recreated the image of his face in my head and stared into those two pools of baby blue, searching for a splash of red-hot desire. Had he been born a decade or two earlier, surely he already would have been strictly past tense only.

    When I lost Shane, I didn't just lose the guy. I lost what he represented: youth and what part of me must have felt was one final attempt to recapture it. He was still young. His heart would go on because it had only half the wear and tear of mine. He had everything to look forward to. I had too much to reflect on. Was that the curse of being a guy of a certain age, feeling too haunted by the past to forge too bravely ahead into the darkness of the future? I'll take the fearlessness, the shining light of youthful abandon, thank you very much.

If my time with Shane produced any new dating rules, they had less to do with the type of person I'd date in the future than how I'd fight with him. Important conversations should be had in person, not by email or text. Shane and I had conducted too many big talks the modern way when we should have communicated face to face, or over the phone when we were on different continents.

I half-suspected that if we'd had our heated back-and-forths in real time, while reading each other's facial expressions and body language and responding to them, our breakup conversations would have ended in hugs instead of goodbyes. I might never know for sure, unless he one day reentered my life again, which was a development that I was no longer secretly expecting.

I wasn't holding out for a hero, whether it be Shane or someone I hadn't yet met. I may not have been completely over him, but my recovery was a work still in progress. My second round of Shane-less months — without rebound dates, without rebound sex — had retaught me a crucial lesson, one that had defined my adult life, one that I'd forgotten while I was clinging to hopeless love: I could make it on my own. In some ways, I was better off alone. The way

I had begun my life abroad was the way I would continue it.
   This state of independence shall be. This state of independence shall be.
   No matter where my road leads.

Epilogue: Understanding

They call it understanding, a willingness to grow. — Bob Seger

The grand epiphany, the culmination of seven years of personal growth, arrived two days into my South African debut, after four months spent traveling through United Arab Emirates, Germany, Poland, Italy, Israel, Palestine and Jordan (with one month apiece in Berlin, Rome and Tel Aviv). I was at the Apartheid Museum in Johannesburg on a Friday afternoon, fully engrossed in a permanent exhibit dedicated to the 1967 book *House of Bondage,* photographer Ernest Cole and writer Thomas Flaherty's beautiful brutal photojournalistic documentation of Apartheid in South Africa. As I stood there with tears welling in my eyes, I felt this unsettling sense of déjà vu. I'd seen those images before — not the same pictures, but ones just like them.

I'd been bombarded with them all my life — in stories I'd been told, in chapters of history books I'd read, on pages I'd pored over in encyclopedias, in movies I'd sat through uncomfortably, all of which revolved around Civil Rights in the United States. The travesties of the Civil Rights era on one side of the world had been committed concurrently with the travesties of Apartheid on the other side of the world, as depicted in Cole's *Bondage* photos.

I suddenly felt connected to South Africa, to Africa, in a

way I'd always been told I should, because I'm black, because it was the ancestral home of my forefathers. As I stared at one image in particular, a black-and-white photo of a little boy melting in the sweltering heat of a township classroom, struggling to concentrate, I saw myself. I never had to study under those difficult conditions, but I thought I knew exactly how he felt: awkward, uncomfortable, stifled, eager to learn. I wondered where he is now. If he *is* now. An old but new thought crept into my mind: We are the world. We are *one* world. For the first time in my life, Africa truly felt like the motherland. It had nothing to do with black pride and everything to do with what I saw in the eyes of that little boy: myself.

That was the moment when I began to suspect that my time in South Africa might be a period of intense healing and self-acceptance. I was already beginning to feel more comfortable in my own skin (self-acceptance), partly because, for the first time in my seven years abroad, when a nonblack person looked at me for too long, I actually had to wonder why. It wasn't because they so seldom saw people with my coloring. It wasn't out of curiosity (Is it true what they say about black men?). It was likely for something that was uniquely me and belonged to me only.

My relationship with black people, who had been largely absent during my seven expat years in South America, Australia and Asia, was changing, too, thanks to my time in Johannesburg. In yet another "you get what you're not looking for" twist, it was never my intention to visit Johannesburg. But when I started looking for flights to Cape Town from the Middle East, the cheapest ones (on Qatar Airways) all went through South Africa's largest city, so I decided, rather than to quickly pass through, I'd linger for five days. I was so glad I did.

In Johannesburg, being around such a large and diverse black population, I felt a certain camaraderie with my fellow black people, a level of comfort that I'd never enjoyed around black people anywhere else. They didn't look at me as if I were an enemy. I couldn't imagine they would ever ridicule the West Indian accent that I had never lost completely. They spoke English with an exotic accent, too!

With my burgeoning newfound appreciation and acceptance of my blackness came a shift in my awareness of it. It crept up on me every time I sat down in a restaurant in Johannesburg. When I went from restaurant to restaurant on 7th Street in the suburb of Melville during my five days there and I saw mostly black staff, it was hard for me not to feel pangs of guilt.

Were the owners, like the proprietors of Lucky Bean, the restaurant next to the Saffron Guest House where I was staying, white? Did the black employees commute to and from the townships of Soweto to earn minimal wages? Who were the invisible occupants of all the beautiful homes in Melville? Was it possible that the black employees worked for black bosses who went home at night to the middle-class houses in the neighborhood?

I hated that I was even asking those questions. I never would have done that in the United States because the division of labor in the restaurants there didn't appear to be determined along white-black color lines. Most of the people who served me were white, and I never wondered where they lived.

It didn't matter that most of the clientele in Melville was black as well, though it mattered more when the clientele wasn't. Which raised another question: Why did white people in Melville flock to certain places on 7th Street and not to others? Why was I dwelling on this stuff?

I supposed it was my personal version of white liberal guilt, the seeds of which may have been planted on the way back from the Apartheid Museum when Solly, my black South African taxi driver, explained the difficulties that blacks continue to face when applying for white-collar work in Johannesburg. I never thought liberal guilt looked particularly good on white people, and it wasn't doing me any favors.

At least I owned it, which I figured was the first step in overcoming this looming new color awareness. I hoped my ongoing evolution in South Africa, in life, would lead not only to complete comfort in my own skin but perhaps, at last, it wouldn't matter to me what color anyone else's was either.

That wasn't exactly what I was looking for when I set out

on my journey, but you get what you're not looking for. Back then I was still more concerned with how other people saw me than how I felt about myself. I didn't know it, but a change was gonna come. Enlightenment: Here it was — at last. After seven years spent wandering, wondering, I was finally understanding, on the cusp of finding a greater love than I'd ever imagined.

Printed in Great Britain
by Amazon.co.uk, Ltd.,
Marston Gate.